VALDERRAMA
THE FIRST TEN YEARS
1985-1995

When the Club was formed in 1985, this noble group of cork oaks by the 2nd green provided the new owner with inspiration for the now-familiar Valderrama logo.

Valderrama
The First Ten Years
1985-1995

The Making
of Spain's
Ryder Cup Course

Jaime Ortiz-Patiño

VALDERRAMA

ACKNOWLEDGEMENTS

I am indebted to many persons for assistance in the
preparation of this book. In particular I would like to thank
Phil Sheldon for his fine photographs of the golf course and
of the Volvo Masters winners. Other photographs are owed to
the Royal Society for the Protection of Birds; to Martin
Jacoby, who also contributed the appendix on wildlife;
to Doro; to the late Raymond Gardner and to Peter Realf.
Titus Kendall, curator of the Club museum, and Eva Seitz-
Kolm, my secretary, were most helpful, and I have borrowed
liberally from the thoughts and writings of Robert Trent Jones,
the golf-course architect. However, this book would not have
been possible without the assistance and hard work of Peter
Dobereiner and Albert Dormer.

I also take this opportunity to acknowledge the example set by
the Andalucian Golf Federation and the Royal Spanish Golf
Federation, whose work for golf in Spain has been a constant
inspiration to me.

ISBN 0-9526131-1-5

BRITISH LIBRARY CATALOGUING IN PUBLICATION DATA.
A CATALOGUE RECORD FOR THIS BOOK IS AVAILABLE FROM THE
BRITISH LIBRARY.

PUBLISHED BY JAIME ORTIZ-PATIÑO, LONDON

FIRST PUBLISHED 1995

DESIGN AND COMPUTER ILLUSTRATION BY PROJECT GRAPHICS,
BASINGSTOKE, HAMPSHIRE, ENGLAND

TYPESETTING, IMAGESETTING AND PRINTING BY
TURNERGRAPHIC LIMITED, BASINGSTOKE, HAMPSHIRE,
ENGLAND

DISTRIBUTED BY CLUB DE GOLF VALDERRAMA
11310 SOTOGRANDE, PROV. DE CADIZ, SPAIN

CONTENTS

VALDERRAMA

HOW I CAME TO OWN VALDERRAMA

Those who think ownership of a golf course by an individual can be merely a rich man's pastime are not very perceptive – and they almost certainly are not golfers. I knew when I became involved with Valderrama that I was making a commitment, even a dedication, to a whole way of life.

In the early 1980s my life was at a turning point. I was winding down a hectic seven-days-a-week business career and would no longer be a slave to air-line schedules. My philanthropic interests were active, not just contributory, and my fine-art collection took some attention, but they could not fill my time. I was still president of the World Bridge Federation but after ten often-turbulent years I had achieved my goals and the post would now seem less exciting to me. I had already resolved not to stand for a fourth term in 1986.

Also, I found myself becoming increasingly attached to Spain, especially Andalucia, and I wanted to spend much more time there. I had been one of the first to build a house on the Sotogrande estate in the late 1960s. My villa was on the Old Course and my golfing friends and neighbours were congenial, as were the summer and Easter visitors who came for polo and tennis as well as golf. But one had to wonder how long the idyll could last.

Sotogrande had been started in the 1960s by Colonel Joe McMicking, ex-US Army: his widow Mercedes Zobel, a lovely person, still lives a stone's throw from me in another of the first houses built on the estate. Joe had won international recognition for his exclusive and sensitive developments in the Philippines and knew that to repeat the formula in Spain he would need beautiful countryside, coastal access, enough land – thousands of acres – to ensure that the environment was protected, and above all, adequate water supplies. He told his wife's nephew, Alfredo Melian, to get on his motor-bike and travel north, south, east and west until he found such a place. Joe added that there must also be enough suitable land between the coastal road and the sea for a first-class golf course.

VALDERRAMA

'Freddie' rode far and wide and eventually found a group of three *fincas,* or country estates, that met the requirements and had no new development for many miles around. They were called Sotogrande, Paniagua and Valderrama. Joe acquired these properties and started to service them with roads. He brought in his friend, the great American golf architect, Robert Trent Jones, to lay out a very fine golf course. Joe had to give a name to his new development, and as he had not finalised the purchase of Valderrama he decided on the name Sotogrande. His golf course therefore became Club de Golf Sotogrande, sometimes referred to as the Old Course. Then, gradually, he sold large plots for the building of individually-designed houses.

The name Sotogrande became a byword for quality and a fashionable address for the international set, but by the early '80s the development of the Costa del Sol westwards from Marbella had gathered a seemingly unstoppable momentum. Could the estate withstand the tide of concrete? Joe was talking of retirement and the day must come when he would hand over the management to others, whose objectives might differ.

And so at this time I felt vaguely disquieted. I wanted to do something to preserve the status quo – but I couldn't think of anything constructive. Then, thanks to one of my regular golfing companions, my thoughts began to focus.

Paul Jeanty is a retired Belgian banker and a fellow-resident on the Sotogrande estate. We had played many enjoyable rounds together on the Old Course, strolling across the lawns of my villa in the early morning straight onto the 4th tee, long before anyone was about. At the rest hut by the 10th tee we would pause for a breakfast of hard-boiled eggs and vodka and orange brought to us by my faithful Paco Paco, who would pedal alarmingly along the *Paseo del Parques* with the goodies balanced on his handle bars. In the early years we would reach the 18th green before there was any real traffic on the 1st tee and we were able comfortably to play holes 1, 2 and 3, finishing up at my villa.

VALDERRAMA

Pioneers of the Valderrama tradition. From the left: founder member George S. Moore, Henry Cotton, Pierre Crokaert and developer Joe McMicking.

If this account brings a smile to the reader who suspects, rightly, that at Valderrama today such irregularity would call down the wrath of the Club president, I can only plead the sentiment of a Latin tag, dimly remembered: 'Times change and we must change with them.'

Both Paul and I realised that smaller plots, apartment buildings, and the influx of many new residents would mean a more crowded Old Course and a threat to our peaceful and harmonious golfing lifestyle. Then one morning early in 1984 Paul said, 'Why don't you buy Las Aves and run it as a very exclusive private club for yourself and your friends?'

Las Aves, opened in 1975 and originally called Sotogrande New, was situated away over on the other side of the coastal highway. Like the Old Course it had been designed by Robert Trent Jones, whom I and many others considered the world's greatest living golf architect. It and the extensive areas around it had been part of the

The Maestro *in exile at Las Aves. Henry Cotton enjoyed sanctuary as director of golf.*

VALDERRAMA

Valderrama *finca* that had been acquired by Joe McMicking a little after the other two.

Joe had intended Las Aves as the lure that in due time would attract buyers for the real-estate lots around it. It was run more as a golfing facility than as a club, although it had a delightful clubhouse in the Andalucian style that served also as a cinema for the local residents and their children on Sundays. Henry Cotton when exiled by a revolution in Portugal had been welcomed by Joe to act as golf director and to help with the promotion of real-estate sales on this new part of the estate. When Henry returned to Portugal it came under the direction of Tony Jacklin. I was fully convinced that the golf course had the potentiality for greatness if certain defects could be remedied.

The idea of my own golf course where I could aim for the highest standards appealed strongly, and not just for reasons of personal enjoyment. My golfing background was originally British, from early associations with The Berkshire, but years of travel within the United States had introduced me to many of the very best golf courses. Between the two I had firm ideas as to what a golf course should be like and how a golf club should be run.

Golf in Spain was on the move, thanks at first to the impact of such professionals as the Miguel brothers and Ramon Sota, and then of Severiano Ballesteros, whose fabulous successes had fired the public's imagination. I felt that it would be a real service to Spanish golf and those who were working to promote the game if there were to be one golf course in Spain to equal the best in the world and serve as a model.

Also, running a golf course would give scope for another of my interests. As a member of the 1001 Club of the Worldwide Fund for Nature I was deeply committed to the preservation of natural habitats and the conservation of wildlife. With my own golf course I could do something positive to further my belief in the benefit of green areas to human society. But could I get Las Aves on suitable

terms? I could foresee all kinds of difficulties in the way of a deal.

It was known that Las Aves was discreetly on the market and that others were interested too. The Sotogrande estate was no longer under the control of Joe McMicking, who had passed ownership to the Zabel-Ayala group, members of his wife's family. The speculation was that their company, Financiera Sotogrande, was willing to dispose of certain assets because it wanted to dress up the balance sheet. However, it seemed to me that the golf course was the vortex of powerful economic forces that it would be dangerous to underestimate. It was ringed by what would soon be prime and more-than-prime building land, and I had no intention of acquiring a golf course that would be the sugar-plum in someone else's cake. At the same time, I did not want to go into the real-estate business, so there had to be a limit to the amount of expensive land I was prepared to buy to protect the course.

Moreover, some key 'island' plots had already been sold and would definitely have to be repurchased, as their development would block a redesign of the golf course and would also have a devastating effect on its character.

I had to reconcile these difficulties with the fact that the acquisition of Las Aves would satisfy me only if I could be sure that the golf course itself would continue to enjoy a beautiful environment.

I thought it over and figured out some solutions that might work. Then I told Paul that I would be interested in buying Las Aves but would put up only 50%. He was puzzled. 'Why only 50%?', he asked, knowing that resources were not a major problem.

I was well aware that the purchase of high-profile property by foreigners can be an emotive issue in any country – and Andalucians are an especially proud people. They do not accept incomers, even from other provinces of Spain or other parts of Andalucia, with any ease. In my heart I did not see myself as a foreigner, but my family's ancestral links with Spain were several generations removed and therefore I did not want to appear in a dominating role. When I explained

Robert Trent Jones was considered by many, including me, to be the world's greatest living golf architect.

this to Paul he immediately replied: 'That's no problem. We'll form a consortium.'

Paul proceeded to bring in four persons, including himself, who had homes on, or who frequently visited, the estate: Sir Philip Oppenheimer, former chairman of De Beers; Rainer Gut, chairman of Crédit Suisse; and Helmut Maucher, chairman of Nestlé. I also asked George S. Moore, former president and CEO of Citibank, to join our consortium, which he did immediately. Nobody could say we were not serious people. I also enlisted another dear friend who stood no less well with Dun & Bradstreet than the rest of us. Jacques (Kiko) Bemberg, the head of a leading Argentinian family that had known mine for generations. He agreed to acquire up to 15%, a holding that would later prove pivotal.

We were still 15% short but by this time Financiera Sotogrande were eager to proceed and their president, Enrique Zobel, another nephew of Mercedes McMicking, personally put up the balance.

Henry Cotton's tyre drill called for strenuous exercising of right and left hands.

This was the easy part: before a deal could be struck there would be obstacles to be overcome. My colleagues left the negotiations in my hands and I developed a strategy. First I had to speak to the course architect: the golf course had to be redesigned, and I could not imagine engaging anyone other than Robert Trent Jones to redesign a Trent Jones course. Would he sympathise with my proposals, and would he take on the job? He was at the pinnacle of his profession, no longer young, and not in need of work. I called him up in Florida and his reaction was all that I could have desired.

As I had expected, he told me that the shortcomings I had noticed in the golf course were due to a tight budget originally and to the retention for later residential development of certain key plots that were vital if we were to transform Las Aves into a great golf course. 'I have designed enough courses not to ask for the moon,' he told me, 'so I went along with it. And anyway, I was still very pleased with my design.'

'If I can get those plots,' I asked him, 'and if I can give you an open-ended budget, will you redesign the course the way you would originally have wanted it?' He responded very positively, saying that he strongly favoured the redesign and would thoroughly enjoy working with me on it.

Thus there started for me a new and lasting friendship with a great man, a golf architect of genius, and with his charming wife and two very talented sons who were following in their father's footsteps, Robert Trent Jones Jr. and his younger brother Rees Jones.

Next I went back to Financiera Sotogrande. 'The deal is on,' I told Enrique Zobel, 'provided that the plots I need for a redesign of the course are included.' I also told him that certain important building lots adjoining the golf course would also have to be included, for in no other way could we ensure the sympathetic development of this land in the fullness of time.

These matters were agreed and the problem of water rights was also sorted out, but we were still not home and dry. Local zoning ordinances would allow certain of the lands that remained in

the ownership of Financiera Sotogrande to be developed at an unacceptably high density, and we asked Financiera Sotogrande to agree to a lower density. After a certain amount of haggling the company saw our point of view and with the concurrence of the local authority the desired zoning changes were made.

By mid-1985 the negotiations were successfully concluded and our little consortium proceeded to form two Spanish companies: the first, Valderrama SA, would hold the land on which the golf course was built, including the parcels needed for the redesign, and would lease it to the soon-to-be-formed not-for-profit sporting association called Club de Golf Valderrama, each member of which on entry acquires a 'B' share in Valderrama SA.

The second company, Inmobiliaria Sotoalto SA, would acquire and hold building land adjoining the golf course that we would expect ultimately to develop ourselves or dispose of for private houses. Each member of the consortium would hold the same percentage of shares in Sotoalto SA as in Valderrama SA, and would become a Founder Member of the Club de Golf Valderrama. The Club was incorporated in June 1985 with Joe McMicking as Honorary President, and a month later was granted a lease until 2010 at a fairly nominal rent. The first annual general meeting was held at Easter, 1986.

I myself chose the name Valderrama, and after ten years I am still happy with it. It commemorates the name of the *finca* that Joe had acquired a little after the other two. 'Had I been able to buy the Valderrama estate at the start,' Joe told me years afterwards, 'I would have called the whole shebang Valderrama instead of Sotogrande.'

Joe died in 1990 aged 82 and I felt that his last years were happier because he knew that at Valderrama we would perpetuate his dream of excellence.

I was very pleased to find that although our purchase of the golf course had caused a considerable stir in Sotogrande, there was no adverse reaction from the indigenous people, including the villagers of nearby Guadiaro,

Torreguadiaro and Tesorillo, who formed the backbone of our maintenance staff. After less than a year working with them I knew that I was *persona grata* and that my reluctance to take full ownership had been unduly cautious. Perhaps my Spanish ancestry – and being able to speak their language – had helped me after all.

And indeed, it was not long before the matter of ownership became somewhat of a problem. The redesigning of the golf course required fresh capital over and above the money generated by the sale of shares. The Founder Members had assumed a financial burden and given freely of their time in order to enjoy playing on a lovely golf course with their friends, but this objective was now assured and they were content.

Instead of putting up more money, they hoped to see a return on money already invested, so they quite rightly felt we should activate our real-estate potential, by way of Inmobiliaria Sotoalto SA, the holding company. This was done by inviting Enrique Perez Flores, the president of Banco Exterior (Suiza) SA, to join our group and

HRH The Prince Andrew, Duke of York, Honorary Member.

giving him executive responsibilities as well as equity participation by way of a 25% increase in the Company's capital. I felt I had to go along with this, so my 50% went down to 40%, Kiko Bemberg's 15% went down to 12%, and so on.

I soon realised that the objectives now being pursued by Sotoalto SA did not sit well with my own wish to protect the golf course. Matters came to a head when it was proposed to erect five 3-storey apartment buildings on a site a stone's throw to the right of the Clubhouse, obliterating the view from the Clubhouse terrace of the sea and of the 11th green. This is the linchpin site that has been occupied in recent years by the Volvo hospitality tents, and that has been earmarked for the Hospitality Village for the 1997 Ryder Cup. I could scarcely believe it – but then I found that the proposal was serious, some of the apartments already having been sold off plan!

When I recovered my poise I had all the Club's flag poles shifted to a position where they would mark out the building line of the proposed blocks. Then I had them joined at the top with a wooden fascia to indicate the intended height. It was Easter, 1988, a time when Members are present in their greatest numbers. They must have thought I had gone out of my mind and given permission for some kind of sleazy advertisement hoarding. 'Is this what you want to see when you look out of the Clubhouse?', I asked the Founder Members. Two of them were as appalled as I was, and with their votes to add to mine the proposal was dead in the water. But all eight Founder Members agreed that we should come to a friendly arrangement to overcome the problem of different objectives.

The suggestion was made that my 40% of Sotoalto SA should be exchanged for the three key sites most vital to the preservation of amenity. The basis of valuation was fair, but I did not like the idea of a commercially-driven Sotoalto SA in different hands from Valderrama SA. I thought it over and made a counter-offer: I would buy their 60% holding in Sotoalto SA on the basis of the same valuation and I would also buy all the

My wife Uta and I always enjoy the company of HRH Prince Bernhard of The Netherlands

Founder Members' shares in Valderrama SA at their investment-cost plus interest.

The offer was accepted and in June 1989 I assumed 100% control of Sotoalto SA, the name of which I changed to Valderrama Estates SA, and acquired all the shares in Valderrama SA other than the 'B' shares owned by the Members. The value of the Members' shares was heavily underpinned: no matter how much more capital I myself invest in Valderrama SA committed to the golf course, the 500 'B' shares rank for 50% of the net assets in event of liquidation. I also undertook to cover the Club's considerable annual operating deficit until June 30, 1999.

Matters were, I felt, at last on an even keel. Thanks to the forbearance of the Founder Members, I had been able to recover from the mistake of not taking outright ownership initially. For introducing partners of such calibre I had to thank Paul Jeanty.

Now I could turn all my attention to the golf course itself. I knew that my far-reaching plans would not always enjoy a smooth ride from the

Dona Emma Villacieros de Garcia-Ogara

VALDERRAMA

Club Members, but I consoled myself with the thought that all the happiest and best-run golf clubs are one-man shows. Given a free hand an individual can immerse himself totally in the job and pursue a consistent and coherent policy. The members know where they stand. If they approve, that is fine. If they disapprove they can move to another club more congenial to their tastes.

An outstanding example of a one-man club is Augusta National, home of The Masters. The golf course itself was inspired by the legendary Bobby Jones in the Thirties, but the practicalities of raising the funds in the middle of the Depression and bringing the scheme to fruition were left to his friend, Clifford Roberts, who as chairman exercised tight control over every aspect of the running of the club. Even Jones, the president, deferred to him in matters of administration. Later chairmen of Augusta have exercised a similar monopoly of power.

Pine Valley, widely acclaimed as the world's Number One golf club, has a nominal committee but is effectively run by the president. This arrangement came about through the sheer force of personality of John Arthur Brown, whose habit was to put his proposals to the committee with the words, 'Those in favour say 'Aye'. Those against say 'I resign'.' I intended to follow the example of Roberts and Brown, not out of hubris but because I was thoroughly convinced that it was the best way to achieve the highest standards and a like-minded membership. If I failed I would have no one to blame but myself.

It had been a tough struggle but now at last I was able to realise my dream of creating a great golf course. How I set about it is described in the next chapter.

VALDERRAMA

The new lake at the 17th, cunningly sited to tempt the golfer to go for the green with his second shot, provides moments of high drama for spectators.

HOW VALDERRAMA BECAME NUMBER ONE IN EUROPE

The task facing me was not that of transforming an ugly duckling into a swan. Valderrama was already a course of quality, in no way a poor relation to its companion Sotogrande down the hill. And its natural advantages were many. It lies in ideal terrain between the stark grandeur of the Sierra Blanca mountains and the Mediterranean, with distant views of Gibraltar and North Africa from the higher ground. Its gnarled old cork oak trees are typical of this part of Spain. It also has numerous olive trees, and wild flowers in abundance.

When Robert Trent Jones made the first of his trips to discuss and supervise the redesign he did not conceal his enthusiasm. 'I am in the favourable position,' he told me, 'of being able to do the things I might have wanted to do earlier – and to do them with knowledge of how the course has developed its own character since then, in the way golf courses do.'

He contributed his experience and creative force without stint and we spent many happy days together, going round the course and discussing where and how improvements could be made.

We had a clear idea of what we wanted:
1. A course that would fully extend the world's best players but would also set attainable goals for the club golfer.

'The alchemists had similar objectives,' Trent Jones told me, 'but it can be done. Every hole should be a difficult par and an easy bogey.' This was achieved by having a range of tees differentiated not just by distance but by good siting. A group of trees may present a much more serious hazard from the back tees than from the front. We would have four tees for men and two for ladies. To enjoy your game you should choose the right tee to suit your handicap.
2. A very highly maintained course, like Augusta National and others in the USA, with relatively narrow and contoured fairways.
3. Championship Pencross greens, fast and firm, reading 9½' to 10½' on the stimpmeter for members, increasing to 11.0' to 11½' for championships.

4. Punishing rough bordering the Bermuda 419 fairways, 1½" for membership play, 2½" for championships.

5. 2" roughs around the greens, a mixture of rye grass and creeping bentgrass.

6. Semi-rough only the width of one Triplex mower, both around the fairways and around the greens.

7. Bunkers smooth and firm.

8. No *poa annua* on the course. *Poa annua* is not pernicious but it is much inferior to creeping bentgrass as it does not provide a true and uniform putting surface. It invades after a couple of years all but the most highly-maintained golf courses, and Valderrama is the only course I know on this side of the Atlantic that is virtually free of it nearly all the year round.

I do not like the idea of unlimited budgets, mindful as I am of the client who remarked in mock dismay of the golf-course architect Pete Dye: 'I gave him an unlimited budget – and he exceeded it!' But I did tell Trent Jones to let his imagination slip the collar of financial restraint

Could that possibly be a weed I spy through my binoculars? Robert Trent Jones, relaxing on the cart, seems confident that I must be mistaken.

and explore the possibilities of an ideal world in which money was a secondary consideration. He did not let me down.

We resolved to make most of the necessary changes during the first three years. I will mention here only the major ones. (A list of alterations appears in Appendix IV.) First, the re-purchase of the vital 'island' plots enabled us to remodel the 11th green, as well as the 12th, 15th and 16th tees, improving the shot values in each case. The 4th, the hole furthest from the Clubhouse, was completely rebuilt, Trent Jones stating with pride that it would win recognition as one of the best of all his par 5s. With its lake and cascade the 4th cost the earth, but in the same year, 1988, we contrived a brilliant change that cost nothing: we re-numbered the course, making the first hole 10, the second 11, the tenth 1, and so on. (Throughout this book I use the new numbering, regardless of the date of which I am writing.)

Why was this such a bright idea? First, the old 1 to 9 were the more testing holes and therefore

The cascade alongside the 4th green is the most photographed feature on the course. I do not care for the idea of a designated 'signature hole' but I suppose if Valderrama had to have one this would be it. It certainly offers the golfer a beautiful prospect although (see pages 21 and 22) less appealing if he has hit his approach this far through the green.

It took rather more than faith to move the mountain of earth required to level the practice ground and make it one of the best training amenities to be found anywhere.

deserved to form the inward nine. The old 9th hole was the best par 4 on the course, as good a finishing hole as you could possibly wish for. It was also well suited to the formation of spectator mounds – far more pleasing to the eye than grandstands, and another reason why it would make an ideal 18th.

Moving from the new 9th green to the 10th tee brings you past the Clubhouse, obviating the need for a halfway house elsewhere on the course. And finally, the new first hole was brought nearer the putting green, allowing those waiting to tee off to practice their putting while keeping the first tee in view.

These improvements left us with only one hole of less than championship quality: the 17th, which Peter Dobereiner once described as a long, slogging par 5 where the only requirement is to move the ball forward. When it had been the 8th, this had not mattered so much, but now its lack of character was all too obvious.

Transforming the hole was a mammoth task involving changes to the fairway contours, the

VALDERRAMA

This picture shows two greens at the 4th hole but the one in the background will be taken out before the Ryder Cup, together with the two bunkers on its left.

formation of a lake and stream, the building of a
new green and tees, and the extension of the
gabion walls near the green. The lake was put in
on Trent Jones's recommendation but he was
unable to supervise the construction and at his
suggestion his concept was carried out by
Severiano Ballesteros. The 17th is now a
spectacular hole where the green can be reached
in two by an adventurous player who carries the
lake with his second shot. Spectators have fine
views, either from the natural amphitheatre
behind the green, from which you look across
the lake and see the players advancing towards
you, or from various levels of the gabion walls.

By this time I understood Trent Jones's design
philosophy and was confident I could see to it
that when adjustments to Valderrama were
needed, they would be made in keeping with our
distinguished 'designer label'. For example, while
the work of Seve's design company on the 17th
was highly successful, it seemed to my eye
incongruous in one small way: the bunkering
behind the green did not have the authentic

*Plenty of trouble at the 7th where a long approach shot must
fly what might appear to be the result of a comprehensive
carpet-bombing raid.*

Trent Jones look. His preference is for tongues of turf and irregularities in the outlines of his hazards. And so the 17th was adjusted accordingly.

With the completion of the new 17th just before the 1993 Volvo Masters, Valderrama now had four magnificent finishing holes.

Of course, we made many improvements that are not obvious to the casual observer, notably to drainage. Valderrama can now look the most freakish weather conditions in the eye. The winter of 1989 saw more than two months of phenomenal rainfall, but while every other well-known course on the Costa was closed for several weeks, Valderrama was closed only for four days during November, December and January.

While busy with Trent Jones on the redesign of the course I was active on another front also. A championship course must have a skilled work force, using the most modern equipment under the direction of a golf-course superintendent who thoroughly understands each man's job, who is highly skilled in turf-grass management, and is

adequately informed in such matters as agronomy, drainage, arboriculture, and so on.

I was determined to be that superintendent. I felt I could do the job, and with my insights into the Andalucian character I was sure I would have a better relationship with my work force than an incomer.

So I put myself through a crash course in turf-grass management and allied disciplines, attending courses and seminars in the United States alongside professional golf-course superintendents. They are a great bunch of people. I mixed with them, drank with them, and picked up much extra-curricular information. They were invariably impressed when they found that I was from Spain. 'Gee,' one of them told me, 'your members must be well-heeled if they can send you all this way.' Sometimes I took along our pro, Juan Zumaquero, and I was delighted when he successfully completed the diploma course in turf management at the University of Massachusetts. Juan was my caddy on the Old Course as a boy; now he is my assistant

Valderrama golf course as it is today, showing the Short Course, which was also designed by Robert Trent Jones, and the superb practice facilities.

Short Course

Practice Facilities

VALDERRAMA

superintendent and when I am away is entrusted with maintaining the golf course according to a programme well laid down and revised every six months. He is also a fully-qualified golf-teaching professional endorsed by the Spanish Golf Professionals Association.

Early in 1986 fortune smiled when Bobby Russell, chairman of the USGA Foundation, introduced me to a figure who was to become my guide and mentor in matters of turf-grass

management. William H. Bengeyfield was about to retire from his posts as National Director of the USGA Green Section and chairman of the USGA Turfgrass Research Program. He was available for consultancy work. I found that Bill knew everything there was to know about the care and nurture of top-class golf courses and, no less important, he had the same appetite for perfection as Trent Jones and I. Bill became a regular visitor to Valderrama and with his help I learned, painfully at times, how to keep cool-season grasses alive through the scorching Spanish summer. Bill also helped me to teach the crew their jobs and to compile a new building programme for our tees and greens.

To have first-class greens one should use a single strain of grass expressly developed and hybridised for the purpose. Our variety is from the Creeping Bentgrass family and is called Penncross. It is a cool-season grass which provides the finest of all putting surfaces to play on, but it cannot tolerate extreme conditions, and moreover, monoculture is an unnatural form of

What it takes to guarantee a perfect lie for every shot: the armoured division of maintenance machinery in their livery of Valderrama red.

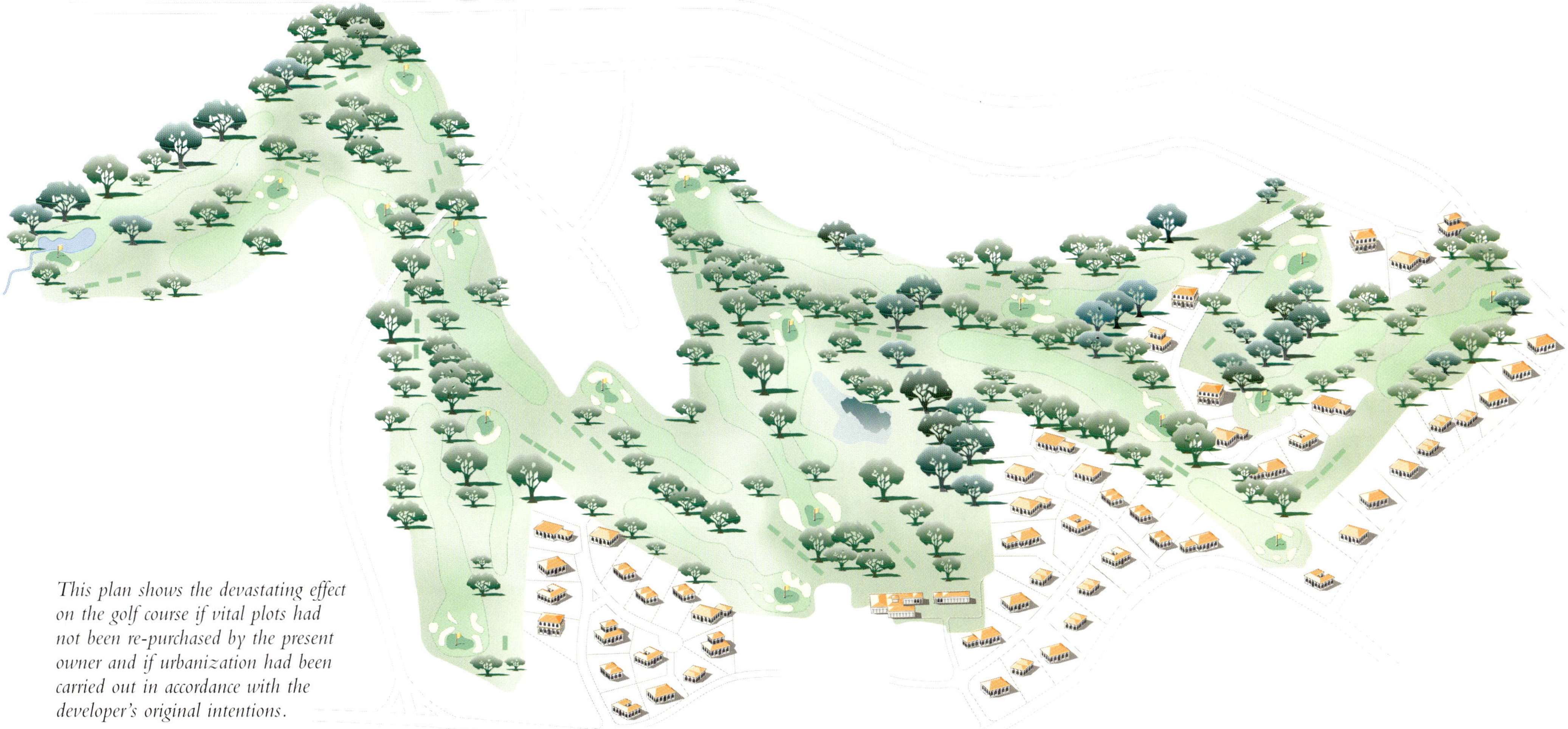

This plan shows the devastating effect on the golf course if vital plots had not been re-purchased by the present owner and if urbanization had been carried out in accordance with the developer's original intentions.

Water loss from a leaking lake is expensive enough to justify a major overhaul, which is what we did to our main irrigation reservoir.

agronomy. To practice it successfully, even under favourable conditions, calls for extreme vigilance.

At Valderrama we have two prevailing winds. The poniente from the parched and arid hinterland is a killer whose hot breath can completely destroy a green in one day. When it blows in the summer, simply to keep the grass alive we must syringe the greens frequently. And it has to be done exactly right, for excessive watering, as every Keeper of the Green knows, carries its own dangers by creating favourable conditions for the invasion of fungal diseases, which can ruin a green in 24 hours, and the encroachment of alien grasses such as *poa annua*. Fortunately the poniente is not humid: if it were, no amount of attention would enable the bentgrass to survive. It simply cannot stand traffic and humidity combined with heat.

Our humid wind is the levante, which comes over the Mediterranean and in the summer brings a cool sea breeze. The levante is not a problem for the Keeper of the Green; only for the player!

VALDERRAMA

The Bermuda grass on our fairways and roughs is altogether different from the bentgrass. It is a warm-season grass, strong and virile, requires little water and is free from chronic diseases. In the cool season it goes semi-dormant and turns off-colour, but then returns in the spring as vigorous as ever.

At Valderrama we lavish great care and attention on our greens. Unless greens are true, putting becomes too much a matter of chance rather than skill. When we rebuild a green we do so strictly according to USGA specifications. And whenever time permits we seed rather than sod the greens. This is more trouble but gives an even better putting surface.

Concerning the speed of the greens, one has to be sensible and flexible. It is good management to place the greens under stress every now and then, as an athlete does to prepare himself for a specific event when he will have to be in peak condition. However, during the rest of the year the greens

The problem of heavy machinery damaging the playing surfaces demanded a radical solution and this is it, the service tunnel under construction out to the 12th green.

The 8th is a short par 4 and after a well placed tee shot requires no more than a pitch to the green, but the distance must be judged precisely to carry the large bunker partly surrounding the green.

have to be kept in a sustainable state: fast, but within reason, and with due consideration for climatic conditions.

For everyday play the members want fast greens, as they have been accustomed to them, but they do not want them as slick as U.S. Open championship greens. On the other hand, for championships, including the Volvo Masters, Valderrama has to adhere to its standards of fast greens, narrow fairways and severe roughs. For the Ryder Cup, the European captain and the Ryder Cup committee will have the greens at whatever speed they choose, and the roughs and fairways likewise.

I know of only one course in Spain that has better greens. In 1991 we opened our nine-hole par 3 course, which is integral with the main course and was also designed by Robert Trent Jones. It is a peach of a short course. Each green was constructed under my personal supervision, strictly to USGA specifications and I confess to a warm feeling when Jeffrey Perris, director of the famous Sports Turf Research Institute at Bingley

No, not Lake Geneva but the lake adjoining our 10th hole.

THE PAR-THREE COURSE

Sometimes the smallest gems sparkle with the brightest lustre and by general acclaim that seems to be true in the case of Valderrama's par-three course. It was built in 1991 to a plan sketched by Robert Trent Jones and the work was carried out under the supervision of his associate, David Krause. By this time I had undergone an intensive study course in agronomy with the United States Golf Association's Green Section, putting particular emphasis on the latest developments in the construction and care of greens. I was therefore well versed in the most up-to-date technology and immersed myself deeply in the project. We had the advantage over the greens of the main course of some twenty years of scientific research and development by the USGA, by many universities and their turf grass experimental stations. We were rewarded by the remarks by Jeffrey Parris from the Sports Research Institute at Bingley, Yorkshire, who said: 'In 25 years of studying turf grass around the world I have never seen such greens. Now I know what a green should really be like.' That compliment has since been echoed by innumerable golfers who have been enchanted by the challenge and the grandeur of our sparkling little gem ringed with wild flowers and shrubs.

I must add that I received those compliments about the par-three's greens being 'even better than those on the big course' with somewhat mixed feelings and immediately set in train a programme of rebuilding and up-grading the greens of the par-three's big brother. In the natural way of things they were about due for re-laying anyway.

Pictured here is the longest, most beautiful and most difficult hole, the 2nd.

in Yorkshire, said after a visit: 'In 25 years of studying turf grass around the world, I have never seen such greens. Now at last I know what a green should really be like.'

I am very receptive to suggestions and criticisms from informed quarters. The practice ground was highly thought of but did not serve its purpose quite well enough for some of the more demanding professionals who came to Valderrama for the Volvo Masters. I felt they were right in their criticism, so a vast quantity of fill was brought in to level out the steep downslope, creating a surface similar to most of our fairways. Now players would know from their practice shots how far the ball would really travel. My reward for this labour was to hear Nick Faldo and many others describe the practice facilities as the equal of any in the world.

A thorny problem was the missing link in our network of maintenance roads. Few things are more dispiriting than hitting a good drive onto the fairway only to find the ball in a tractor rut from which the Rules of Golf provide no relief.

This kind of thing is inevitable on a golf course where maintenance requires that heavy equipment be driven over the playing areas. And that is partly why a tunnel was built under the 12th fairway – even though the fairway had to be raised to accommodate it – and another under the raised driving range.

As a result, our members can now safely take a good fairway lie for granted anywhere on the course. These works also enabled us to do away with existing service roads to the right of the 14th fairway and around the 15th green, and gain precious land needed for extensive landscaping to protect the privacy of the course. This was especially important at the 15th green, which is an important focus for TV cameramen.

No golf-course superintendent can keep a course in good condition without a happy, skilful work force, and it will be clear from what I have written that in the climate of coastal Andalucia, time is of the essence: even the shortest delay in applying remedial measures can be literally fatal to the greens. You must therefore have staff on call

The tenth might be termed a triple whammy hole. The lake dominates the golfer's thoughts as he addresses his tee shot and a touch of fade can startle the fish. Safely escape that peril and you may be lulled into thinking that the rest is routine. A fraction short with your approach to the elevated green and your ball can roll back down the slope to your feet. Too strong and you face a white-knuckle shot from the sand.

every day of the year, which is not so easy to arrange.

I realised very early in my career as benevolent despot that a drastic reorganisation of the staffing was needed if the golf course was to be maintained at the level of my aspirations. Religious festivals, public holidays and staff vacations meant that for up to three days at a time there might be nobody available for urgent work. The conventional system of overtime was unsuitable, as it had to be arranged in advance and no one could predict when an emergency, connected usually with climatic conditions, might arise.

I put a novel proposition to the greens staff – those who look after our cool-season grasses, the greens, aprons, collars, rye grass roughs and semi-roughs around the greens. I would pay them for the full 52 weeks of the year if they would agree to work seven days on, seven days off, regardless of holidays.

The long 11th provides an exhilarating view of the Mediterranean and an entrance to the green so narrow that an aerial approach is recommended.

It was a sweet deal all round. The advantages for the Club were that it would have an adequate work force every day of the year, including Easter and Christmas Day, while the balance of the work force would be available on a normal working schedule. All contingencies would be covered and a rational programme of maintenance and reconstruction could be planned. The reduction of overtime would mean that the two-shift system would not greatly increase the wage bill.

For the workers, the arrangement represented the highly acceptable face of capitalism. The Sotogrande estate provides plenty of work for jobbing gardeners and odd-job men, and Valderrama's greens staff are by upbringing and vocation skilled horticulturists, so during their off-weeks they could easily find casual employment if they wanted it. They did not linger long in debate before accepting the new working conditions.

Most of the workers now play golf and, being equipped with the special insight which comes from

actually participating in the sport, they have acquired a level of greenkeeping skills which equals the best. I am immensely attached to them all, and proud of them. They deserve a large share of the credit for the high reputation Valderrama has gained.

Many a flower, the poet says, is born to blush unseen. No doubt there are some golf courses not in the public eye that do not receive the recognition they deserve. This was never a problem with Valderrama. Even before the redesign was complete, our fairways were winning acclaim as the equal of the best in the world, and our greens are now considered to be of similar merit.

On other fronts, too, Valderrama has won speedy recognition and we now play regular friendly matches with four of the world's most famous clubs: Royal St. George's, The Honourable Company of Edinburgh Golfers, Portmarnock and Pine Valley. What really put us on the map in American eyes was when our Club, represented by Jeremy Caplan (capt.), Björn Ronning, Felipe Ortiz-Patiño and

Michael Lovett won the prestigious National Interclub Invitational Championship at the Robert Trent Jones Golf Club near Washington. Valderrama was one of only three clubs from outside the United States that were invited to compete with 18 leading US clubs.

A championship course needs many qualities, and the criteria for *Golf World*'s ranking list of Europe's top 50 golf clubs are carefully set out. Evidently we score well all round, for in 1991, even before we had our new 17th hole, the magazine's widely-drawn panel of judges voted Valderrama as *Numero Uno*. In 1993 they reaffirmed the ranking. We shall try hard to continue to deserve the accolade.

Michael Lovett, Jeremy Caplan (capt.), Björn Ronning and Felipe Ortiz-Patiño put Valderrama well and truly on the map in American eyes when they won the National Interclub Invitational Championship at the Robert Trent Jones Golf Club near Washington, DC. They beat twenty other famous clubs.

The nightingale can enjoy this view of the Clubhouse while we for our part, sitting inside with the windows drawn back to create a twenty yard span open to the balmy night air, can enjoy the nightingale. Symbiosis supreme.

THE CLUBHOUSE AND MUSEUM

We inherited a clubhouse of character; unpretentious yet making a strong impression with its Andalucian lines, cool inviting entrance and Spanish-tiled roofs. It is well sited and offers extensive views over the golf course. A clubhouse to keep and cherish.

And yet it presented a problem. The kitchen and dining room were designed to provide no more than a snack service. This was all right when Las Aves was more a golfing amenity than a full-blown club, but the facilities were inadequate for preparing and serving the range of meals needed by a good golf club: besides, the electricity supply urgently needed rewiring. Since there was no way we could avoid major upheaval, it made sense to take the opportunity to build in other amenities which our members had the right to expect, and for which space was at present lacking.

A refurbishment programme would also allow the fulfilment of another of my dreams: the provision of a purpose-built museum in which to display my personal pride and joy: the Ortiz-Patiño collection of golfing artefacts, fine art, books and memorabilia.

The architect's brief called for enlarging the amount of usable floorspace without losing the style and character of the exterior. This would be achieved by good internal layout, the use of the latest structural techniques, and unobtrusive additions. The design contract was awarded to the Swedish architect, Lars Liedegren, and as a preliminary he visited the finest clubhouses in the United States. His task was complicated by the fact that the building had to continue functioning as a golf clubhouse while the work was going on. An invaluable contribution to the internal design was made by the French architect, Philippe Herouard, who had previously executed a number of commissions for me.

The new Clubhouse was formally opened at the 1992 Volvo Masters and drew all-round praise. Members now enjoy all the facilities that properly belong to a high-class golf club. (We have absolutely no intention of being mistaken for a country club!) There is a

VALDERRAMA

television room; a snooker room; a bridge room; a bar and refreshment room, accessed as you come off the 18th green or pass from the 9th green to the 10th tee; greatly improved locker rooms; a spacious dining room worthy of the good food now on offer; a wine cellar and new kitchens. The dining room has floor-to-ceiling glazing overlooking the golf course and it can be opened at the touch of a button. Four murals, three of them extensive, embellish the walls of the Clubhouse. They were designed and executed by Robin Archer and Emma Temple Laycock. Two, in the dining room, show general views of the course; another, in the board room, depicts the famous 4th hole.

The fourth mural is in the nature of an artistic joke. The weary golfer who, having finished his round, elects to take the little lift for the short trip to the Club entrance finds that he is a passenger in a balloonist's *pannier*, suspended high above the golf course.

Special praise has been given to the way the architect succeeded in presenting the museum as an architecturally pleasing feature in its own right, while making it an integral part of the building. You encounter it *en passant* when using the Clubhouse and can linger or not, as you please.

The Members contributed about 50% of the costs, excluding the museum area, which is called The Octagon. This was generous of them, as we had only 240 members at that time. I paid the rest, including the costs of the museum area.

The Octagon is a gem. It is accessed by three very short passages that link it to other parts of the Clubhouse. Each passage contains showcases but The Octagon itself – lofty, like an atrium – is the prime position.

One of the first things I did when I became seriously bitten by the golfing bug was to start collecting rare books and artefacts relating to the game. For years, favoured guests at my house might be invited down into the vaults to inspect a veritable Aladdin's cave of golfing treasures: old clubs and balls, pictures and early golf books, many of them still in the packaging of the great auction houses.

When we redesigned the Clubhouse and restaurant we had in mind nothing less than that we should one day have a dining room of genuine gourmet standard. In mid-1995 we gave practical effect to this intention by bringing in a management team that was already responsible for a first-class restaurant near Cadiz. Our joint goal is that Restaurante Valderrama shall attain a similar standard.

The Guide Michelin has never awarded a star to a golf-club restaurant. If it ever does, it is our hope that Valderrama will be the first recipient. And in any case we intend that our cuisine should be of star quality under our distinguished new chef.

Year by year my hoard of golfiana grew as more choice items were purchased privately or at auction, usually through my friend Titus Kendall, a fine-art expert who looks after the museum for me. There was never any mention of the Ortiz-Patiño name, although some of the shrewder dealers and collectors may have suspected the final destination of the prime lots that came onto the market.

Unlike collectors who prefer to gloat in private, I longed for the day when my cherished collection could be examined in detail and at leisure by Members and visitors. The collection is distinguished not by quantity but by relevance and quality. The origins and history of the game of golf are clearly illustrated by the artefacts on display.

My collection includes a unique assemblage of golf balls, beginning with the first true golf balls, the 'featheries'. Some are unmarked, including a very rare red-painted featherball for playing in the snow. There are many examples by the great ball-makers of the 19th century, including two by John Sharp; a ball by Thomas Alexander of Musselburgh; no fewer than three superb

The golfing artefacts on display in the museum area are distinguished not by quantity but by exceptionally high quality. Here are a few of the exhibits, normally displayed in the show cases.

When this gutta ball by Allan Robertson came up for auction in Edinburgh just before the 1992 Open Championship, it was coveted by potential purchasers, both for its importance in the evolution of the golf ball and for the historical fact of its marking Robertson's switch from the featherball. It was therefore expected to attract a world record price - and did.

featherballs by the great ball-maker and golfer, Allan Robertson; and a featherball by the renowned brothers William and John Gourlay.

Perhaps the rarest of all the featherballs is one signed 'McEwan', believed to be one of only two recorded with this stamp. The McEwan family were not generally known as ball-makers, but they had a long historical connection with the Gourlay family. This ball was made to commemorate the death of Peter McEwan and his son in 1836, most probably by John and William Gourlay.

The feather ball was expensive, making golf a rich man's game. When gutta percha was first introduced to Europe in the early 1840s, its suitability for golf balls was very quickly discovered and the first 'gutty' is thought to have been made in 1845 or 1846. Now the featherie was doomed, as the gutty cost only a small fraction of the price. By 1848 its supremacy was assured. The collection clearly charts the changes in the making of the golf ball that so altered the game and broadened its appeal.

VALDERRAMA

The acknowledged master of feather-ball manufacture was Allan Robertson and he vehemently opposed the introduction of the gutty – he even broke off relations with Tom Morris, who had been his apprentice, when he discovered that Morris had been playing with one of the new balls.

But the tide was inexorable and Robertson was no Canute. The collection contains a specimen of great historical importance: it marks Robertson's reluctant conversion to the new-fangled golf ball at a pivotal time in the history of the game. It is unusual in that it is the only ball recorded by Robertson that is randomly hammered, with the intention of enhancing its flight. It is inscribed in ink, 'new kind of golf ball made of gutta percha in the year 1849', stamped Allan, and inscribed 25.

There is a fine group by the legendary Old Tom Morris, including an unused featherball; a hand-hammered gutta percha ball struck with Tom Morris's stamp; another hand-hammered ball and a moulded gutty ball with his own personal stamp, presumably a ball made for his own use, a purpose that so enraged Allan Robertson.

Turning to clubs, there is a display of archetypal Dutch clubs dating from the 15th century, but it is with the advent of golf in Scotland that the strength of the collection is seen. The Scots preferred wooden-headed clubs and golfers carried a selection of them: play club, long spoon, short spoon and putter, complemented by only one iron-headed club for extracting the ball from ruts and similar bad lies. A good selection of rut irons, or track irons as they were sometimes called, can be seen in the museum.

The collection contains examples of wooden clubs by the most illustrious craftsmen, such as Mungo and Willie Park, William and Thomas Dunn, George and David Strath, four generations of the McEwan family, Robert Forgan, James Wilson, Robert Ferguson and five splendid examples by the greatest craftsman of them all, Hugh Philp.

VALDERRAMA

Perhaps the most exciting of the wooden clubs is the superb 18th-century short spoon stamped with the thistle and 'J.McEwan' (for James McEwan, 1747-1800, the founder of the McEwan family business). On the sole of the club is inscribed in ink, 'James McEwan 1786', written in the hand of Douglas McEwan (1869-1929).

Only three clubs thus stamped are recorded as surviving. One, in poor condition and reshafted, is held by the Royal and Ancient. A second and earlier example is in an American collection. The Ortiz-Patiño specimen is the only one of the three that is fully documented, and it ranks as one of the collection's most treasured pieces. It was first recorded in the possession of the McEwan family in an article in the magazine, *Golf*, in 1896 and was exhibited in the 1901 Glasgow Exhibition.

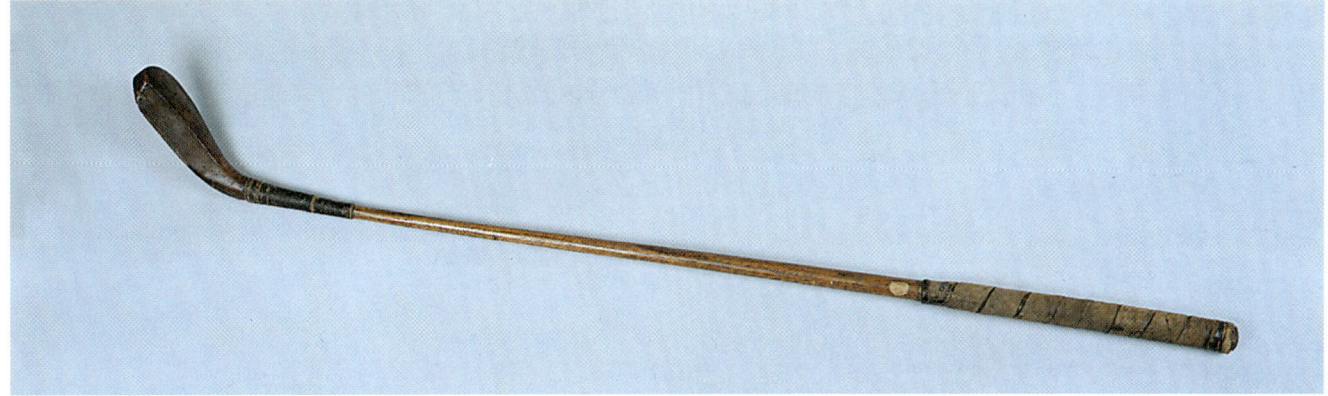

This short spoon by the master craftsman James McEwan, the founder of the family firm, is one of the collection's most treasured pieces and is one of the very few golf clubs still existing that is fully authenticated with tthe maker's name and stamp and that can definitely be attributed to the 18th century. It came originally from the McEwan Family Collection and has been discussed and exhibited for many years.

VALDERRAMA

The evolution of iron clubs is also well portrayed. The oldest is a square-nosed club believed to date from the time of the Act of Union which in 1707 united Scotland with England and Wales. This club is so heavy that it boggles the mind how it could be swung effectively. (It also commanded a notoriously heavy price at auction after being discovered in a carpenter's house in Edinburgh!) Coincidentally, a replica by Peter Dobereiner of an early Dutch club made to the exact size and specification of actual clubheads also produces a finished club of inordinate weight.

My special pride and joy, and not just because it commanded a world record price at auction, is this track iron from the early 18th century. It was found in a cupboard in Edinburgh and is brutally heavy by modern standards.

An extremely rare early 19th-century Spode Imari punch bowl. It is conventionally decorated with peonies and foliage in underglazed blue and reds highlighted with gilt, and has a blue scroll-and-insect decorated border.

The bowl's rarity and interest lie in its being the first known award to an individual of a golf trophy other than a medal, and was given in 1814 by the Bow of Fife Golf Club. Until this time, the trophy played for consisted usually of a silver club that belonged to the Society. Winners would affix to the club a silver replica of the ball they had used, and the club would be retained by the Society.

The proliferation of iron clubs into progressions of different lofts, as well as into weird and wonderful specialist clubs, such as water mashies and frying-pan niblicks, can also be traced in the museum collection.

Among the many items that are of 'museum quality' as works of fine art are three that are very special indeed. The first is the finished oil sketch for what is perhaps the world's most celebrated painting of a golfing subject, and by any measure a masterpiece in its own right. It is *The Golfers* by Charles Lees. Then there is the magnificent Qlanlong punch bowl, one of the very few examples of 18th-century porcelain with a golf motif that survive, and one of the very earliest true works of art relating to the game. The third, of great historic interest, is an early 19th century Spode Imari punch bowl, associated with the Bow of Fife Golf Club, long since disbanded.

The extensive book collection includes many important books, starting with the earliest printed reference to golf: a second edition of the famous *Black Acts*, dated 1566, and a copy of *Golf* by Thomas Matheson, the first printed book devoted entirely to golf.

Since its opening in 1992 the Valderrama museum has acquired an international reputation and has become as much a mecca for golf scholars as Valderrama has for the discriminating player. By rotating the exhibits, some of them kindly loaned by the USGA, continuing interest is assured.

One of my greatest pleasures, when the Clubhouse is quiet, is to pause by some of the choicest pieces, reflecting on the men who created them and who played the game of golf under very different conditions from my Members, but who shared the same values of sportsmanship, restraint and self-discipline.

VALDERRAMA

It is very rare to find any representation of the game of golf on early Chinese porcelain. This Qlanlong porcelain Chinese punch bowl features a medallion that appears also in early letterheads of the Honourable Company of Edinburgh Golfers.
It may therefore have been made for a member who had connections with the East India Company; or perhaps even for the Honourable Company itself. The medallion is taken from a drawing by the genre and portrait painter, David Allan (1744-96), sometimes called 'the Scottish Hogarth.'

VALDERRAMA

The Golf Links, North Berwick, *an oil painting by Sir James Lavery, RA (1856-1941), was made in 1919. Born in Belfast, Lavery was a portrait painter of the Glasgow School. His work, especially his portraits of women, was highly popular. He was knighted in 1918 and elected RA in 1921.*

Landscapes were not his usual subject. This one reflects his love of the game of golf and portrays in affectionate detail a favourite hole at a course of which he was particularly fond and which is still today revered by golfing enthusiasts the world over.

The Golfers *by Charles Lees, RSA (1800-1880), is probably the most important and widely-known of all paintings on a golfing subject. The finished oil sketch for the picture is in the Ortiz-Patiño collection.*

It shows a celebrated encounter on the St. Andrews links in which Sir David Baird and Sir Ralph Anstruther were matched against Major Playfair and John Campbell of Glensaddell. All four were famous players and they shared a military background. The scene is the 15th green on the Old Course. Playfair has just putted and Sir David bends forward with his club in his hand to watch the fate of the stroke.

Enriching the significance of the painting is that among those watching tensely are two of the greatest golf-ball makers, Allan Robertson of St. Andrews (behind Sir David Baird) and William Dunn of Musselburgh (seated, second from right).

The Ortiz-Patiño Collection has strong links with these almost legendary figures: it holds Allan Robertson's historic first gutta ball and the mid-spoon that belonged to him, stamped 'Allan' and made by the famous Hugh Philp. The Collection's link with Dunn consists of a long-nosed club made by him about 1865.

Charles Lees was born at Cupar, Fife, but he settled in Edinburgh. In 1830 he was elected a member of the Royal Scottish Academy and The Golfers *was shown there in 1851.*

VALDERRAMA

Colin Montgomerie stayed two strokes ahead at the 71st hole of the 1993 Volvo Masters and hung on to win by a stroke from Darren Clarke.

THE VOLVO MASTERS

In 1988 there occurred an event that was to have many beneficial consequences for European golf and, as it turned out, very far-reaching consequences for Valderrama too. The PGA European Tour signed a contract appointing Volvo as its main sponsor. Volvo's investment in professional golf has enabled the Tour to introduce new events, guaranteed prize funds and many other improvements, such as courtesy cars for the players and officials at all the Tour events.

The particular element that was to affect Valderrama so much was that, in addition to underpinning the Tour as a whole, Volvo decided that they would sponsor a high-profile tournament of their own. It would be the Tour's annual flagship event and it would also determine the final placings in the season's Order of Merit, with its big cash fund.

The new event would be called the Volvo Masters, and the intention was that it would set a standard of excellence against which other European tournaments would be measured.

Such a strong commitment to quality presented a stiff challenge to Volvo's newly-appointed tour director, Mel Pyatt, a youngish man with the background of a golf pro, plus good business sense and abundant energy. His first priority was to select a golf club and course that would provide a worthy test for Europe's top golfers and that would by its glamour and high presentational standards add lustre to Volvo's image.

To the surprise of all but the shrewdest judges Mel, who was very familiar with the golf courses of the Costa del Sol, plumped for Valderrama. It was a brave choice, considering that in 1988 when the first Volvo Masters was to be held the golf course was still in the throes of redesign, and considering too that I myself had told Mel that the golf course would not be in proper condition until the following year. I took him round and showed him in detail the things we could not do in time, but he stuck to his guns.

The Volvo company backed Mel's judgment and the PGA European Tour also went along with his choice, although there were one or two hurdles to be cleared first. I had had a difference

of opinion with one of the leading pros on the Tour about his habit of throwing down orange peel on the course. Also, a very well-known figure had upset one of my Founder Members, and this too had to be smoothed over. Both of these contretemps were overcome and the Tour declared themselves happy with Mel's choice.

We managed to justify the Sponsor's confidence and by dint of tremendous efforts got the course ready in time. It was a lucky break for me: holding the Volvo Masters at Valderrama had the effect of greatly accelerating international recognition of the Club and the golf course. Even the sternest judges soon had to admit that the leader boards were invariably dominated by strong players, confirmation of the fairness of the course as a championship test.

1994: When golf is pure joy, and pure history.
Bernhard Langer nails a long putt in the 3rd round leading to an incredible course record of 62.

1991: It has been my rigid routine right from the start of the Volvo Masters to rise at 3.30a.m. to greet the greens staff and supervise their pre-dawn labours.

1989: Ronan Rafferty, left, on his way to victory, watches as José-Maria Olazabal cracks one away at the 15th.

In 1988, however, for the lesser lights of the European Tour, their first acquaintance with Valderrama came as a culture shock: they were not used to being set such a searching examination. For the leading players the challenge was much more familiar: narrow fairways, fast and undulating greens which put a high premium on positioning one's approach shots below the flagstick, a course on which you needed to know where the hole was cut before you could plan where to aim your drive . . . this was the golf of the major championship courses in America. Substitute Georgia pines and dogwood for Spanish pines and cork oak and you had a tight Augusta National, not to say a tougher Augusta National when the poniente or the levante blew up strongly.

1988: Nick Faldo.

VALDERRAMA

Sandy Lyle forecast that the winner of this first Volvo Masters would be someone who had experience of play in the United States. He was quickly proved right as he himself, Severiano Ballesteros, Ian Woosnam and Nick Faldo made the running. Faldo was actually the least favoured of the quartet because 1988 had been a frustrating year for him, with only one win and no fewer than eight second-place finishes, including a losing play-off against Curtis Strange for the U.S. Open championship at The Country Club, Brookline. But a storming 68, the only score below 70 on the final day and only the fifth all week, brought Faldo from two strokes behind to a victory by two. 'We defended par,' Trent Jones told me contentedly. He had spent most of the four days in a golf cart watching his favourite art form – the sight of championship players struggling with the problems he had set them – and he was happy with what he saw.

1993, at the 72nd, Montgomerie congratulates Darren Clarke on a fighting finish. 'To be 9 under, as Darren was, and not win is very unlucky,' Montgomerie said afterwards.

VALDERRAMA

1990: Anders Försbrand of Sweden, who is Valderrama's touring professional, shows the style on the 15th tee which earned him the reputation of the finest natural talent on the European Tour.

Severiano Ballesteros taking stock of his putt on the 4th green, in the 1991 Volvo Masters.

In 1989 the winner was Ronan Rafferty. Ireland is a land of highly individual methods, and his two-handed grip and chopping action had excited less comment in amateur golf circles than his supposedly erratic temperament. At the age of 14 he was regarded as an *enfant terrible*, although it seemed that opinions differed as to what made him so *terrible*. The one point on which everyone agreed was that he could play golf. After nine years as a pro he was still only 25 and experienced far beyond his years. He had not made much of a fist of it in 1988, but in compiling a total of 301 he had evidently learnt a lot about Valderrama. This time he tackled the course with great assurance and had the better of a close personal duel with José-Maria Olazabal. He also fought off a challenge from the defending champion, Nick Faldo, and put in a strong finish to win by a stroke on 282. The commentators said that the victory marked Rafferty's professional coming-of-age.

1989: Ronan Rafferty.

VALDERRAMA

1990: Mike Harwood.

In 1990, dominating the tournament right from the start were Bernhard Langer, José-Maria Olazabal, Anders Försbrand, Sam Torrance and the Tour's newest stars, Steven Richardson and Colin Montgomerie. The Australian, Mike Harwood, was also up there, which was no great surprise since he had been a regular winner during his restricted forays into Europe, all his wins being on notably difficult courses. Olazabal took himself out of contention in the third round when he was leading by two strokes. On the 18th his drive finished by a tree and he tried an ambitious left-handed stroke with the club reversed. That cost him a triple bogey and his chance of victory. On the last day the leading pack diminished by a process of attrition. Montgomerie fell out with a 75, while Langer and Försbrand removed themselves with 73s. Then Harwood came home with a 71 to set the target at 286, two over par. If this stood up it would be easily the highest winning score of the

VALDERRAMA

1992: Sandy Lyle plays to the 17th green from a dramatic if unorthodox spot, on the lower shelf of the gabion walls. He made a remarkable shot and holed the putt for a par 5.

1990 European Tour and Harwood was not at all sanguine. But Richardson made bogeys on 16 and 17, and Torrance drove into the fairway bunker on 16, which cost him a stroke to par. Finally the Scot faced a 20-foot putt on the home green to tie Harwood's score. It failed to drop. Everyone had lost except the Australian.

1991 saw one of those paradoxes that help to make golf such a tantalising game. Golf writers have often noted that a golfer will sometimes play better when he has an injury, although it goes without saying that the injury must not be too serious. A pain in the lower back, an ankle sprain, a sore finger, a slight temperature – if you hear a good player complaining about disorders of this nature, then watch out. But what if the player arrives at the tournament on crutches and grimacing with pain following a tennis accident, as in the case of Rodger Davis, the Australian player? Then only a real idiot would risk a bet. Moreover, in an exceptionally strong field Davis

1991: Rodger Davis.

VALDERRAMA

had to contend with among others the consistent Nick Faldo at the top of his form; two great champions in Sandy Lyle and Severiano Ballesteros just coming back to their best form; and Bernhard Langer, the man who had beaten him in a play-off for the German Open three weeks previously. I have heard it said that overseas players – and especially Australians and South Africans – loved odd-numbered years because the Europeans were either preoccupied with getting into the Ryder Cup team or, afterwards, suffering from the trauma of defeat. Times change, and with Europe's vastly improved Ryder Cup performances Davis may have been the last beneficiary of Ryder Cup psychosis with this courageous victory.

In 1992, as the Volvo Masters approached, Sandy Lyle had, according to the commentators, reached a delicate juncture. He had been through a disheartening slump, but he was now beginning to show flashes of his old form. The tournament

1992: Sandy Lyle.

VALDERRAMA

resolved itself into a duel between Lyle and Colin Montgomerie, who was himself suffering from a different form of golfing heebie-jeebies, hitting the ball beautifully but being apparently unable to hand in winning scores. After a succession of close calls this would be his last chance of the year to mount the winner's podium. Both men were therefore under pressure and Montgomerie made things tough for himself with an opening 76, four more than Lyle. Both then had scores of 70, 72 so now Montgomerie really had to assert himself. This he did with a closing 69, while Lyle drifted out to a 73 – and a lucky 73 at that because a shanked 9-iron on the 17th hit a tree out of bounds and rebounded into play. But it was another tree, 60 yards in front of the tee, that vanquished Montgomerie on the first play-off hole, the 10th, Lyle taking the title with a regulation par.

In 1993 Colin Montgomerie handsomely fulfilled the commentators' expectations. In the previous year his battling finish in the US Open

1993: Colin Montgomerie.

VALDERRAMA

championship at Pebble Beach and his tie for a play-off in the Volvo Masters had shown that he had a technique good enough to handle a really tough golf course and a temperament good enough to handle the really big occasion. To win the Volvo Masters and graduate as one of the greatest, all he needed was a fair wind. When Montgomerie played himself into close contention with rounds of 69, 70, 67, his closest rivals were the rising young Ulsterman, Darren Clarke, and the Ryder Cup player, David Gilford – excellent players and well worthy of their exalted positions in the field. Montgomerie during the vital closing stages showed no sign of feeling unduly threatened: he played a beautiful winning round with hardly a blemish, a 68 for a ten under par total of 274. It was, he said, the finest round of golf he had ever played.

The 1994 Volvo Masters, the seventh of the series, was perhaps the most exciting yet. Even before it started, interest was at a new high and

1994: Bernhard Langer.

VALDERRAMA

was boosted by extraordinary events on the golf course. A day without wind is a rarity along the Costa del Sol – and so too was the consequent sight of three players with first-round scores of 65. They were Miguel Martinez, Sam Torrance and Peter Mitchell.

The reaction of some over-excited reporters was that Valderrama had been mastered to the point where it could be humbled by men who had yet to win there, but the truth is that on such a windless day, low scores were not exactly astonishing: indeed Bernhard Langer next day came home with a second round 62, which lowered the course record by three strokes. To add to the drama, Miguel Jiménez delighted the big crowd at the 17th green when he hit a three-iron second shot of 191 metres over the lake and straight into the cup, to add an albatross to the 78 species of birds sighted at Valderrama. The climax came on the final day when Severiano Ballesteros took a two-stroke lead, only to be foiled by Langer at the post to resolve a day that will long be remembered by the fortunate audience.

The 7th Volvo Masters gave me particular satisfaction because it was the very first European golf championship to be televised live by the BBC, whose golf presentations are so much enjoyed. The broadcast was highly successful and augured well for improved media coverage of golf. Adding to my pleasure was the fact that my old friend Peter Alliss, an admirer of our golf course from its earliest days, gave a fine commentary with his colleague Alex Hay. Just two days later I was in London and took a cab from Claridge's to the City. The driver proved to be a keen golfer. He was very talkative and when he found I came from Spain he waxed lyrical about the beauty of a Spanish golf course that he had heard about for years but had never been able to see on television until it was shown by the BBC that weekend. I said not a word, but to this day the cabbie must be wondering why he got quite such a lavish tip.

The Volvo Masters will always hold a place in my affections as the tournament that first enabled Valderrama to demonstrate its qualities to a critical world.

VALDERRAMA

Christy O'Connor and Sandy Lyle on the green of the par-3 6th hole, 1992.

THE KEYS TO VALDERRAMA

In a sporting age of intense and increasing emphasis on money, the Club believes that outstanding achievements should also be honoured by means of the more traditional forms of salutation. Accordingly in 1990 the Club instituted an award for the player with the best three composite performances in the previous three Volvo Masters.

The award takes the form of a ceremonial Key, carved in oak to symbolise the stands of cork oaks which make such a rich contribution to the scenery and the playing strategy of Valderrama. Each year's winner autographs the Key, which hangs in the boardroom. The winner receives a scaled down replica.

More to the point, he also receives courtesy membership of Valderrama for a year and the unlimited use of a fully serviced apartment overlooking the 18th green. This facility has been greatly appreciated by the winners, in particular for family holidays and in winter for taking advantage of Valderrama's unparalleled practice amenities to prepare for the new season's tournament programme.

The Club believes that money is not the only thing that matters to the golfing pro, and that awards based on respect and appreciation still have a part to play.

The value of the award is small in material terms but in may still be seen as meaningful in the human scale.

Winners of the Keys to Valderrama:

1990, José-Maria Olazabal
1991, José-Maria Olazabal
1992, Bernhard Langer
1993, Colin Montgomerie
1994, Colin Montgomerie

José-Maria Olazabal has yet to win the Volvo Masters but his consistent performances have twice earned him the Keys to Valderrama. Will he one day emulate Bernhard Langer? (See next page.)

Bernhard Langer won the Keys to Valderrama in 1992 in a curtain-raiser to taking the Volvo Masters two years later.

In 1993 Colin Montgomerie became the first player to win the Keys to Valderrama and the Volvo Masters in the same year.
The following year he was the easiest-ever winner, his most recent placings being =4th, 1st and 2nd.

Valderrama's environment is shaped by its cork oak trees, and this photograph shows its most celebrated individual specimen. It guards the 5th green on the right of the putting surface: what Robert Trent Jones called his 'bunker in the sky'. The houses shown top right are no longer visible, having been shielded by our planted Halepensis pines.

VALDERRAMA AND THE ENVIRONMENT

Everywhere the environment is under threat, and conservationists are understandably anxious to defend it. At the same time golf continues to attract more and more players who demand more and more golf courses. These interests need not and must not conflict: golfers must convince those who are concerned for the environment that golf is their ally. At Valderrama many members who share this view are supportive of the Club's efforts to protect and enhance our natural surroundings.

The interdependence of golf and the environment is most evident when the golf course is set in wooded terrain: then, the way the golf-course architect and the golf club treat the trees will then be telling evidence of their environmental credentials. The characteristic tree of this part of Spain is the cork, an evergreen species of oak. It is exacting, one might almost say fastidious, in its choice of habitat but when it is happy the tree is hardy and long-lived. Some of our corks may well have been here when Columbus sailed.

Robert Trent Jones laid out the course in such a way as to retain most of the original trees and we have added many more. Our total of 2766 corks includes hundreds that we have planted from a nearby nursery and more than 30 larger corks that we have moved from positions where they would have faced the axe. Our corks are some trouble to us, as their leaves and numerous acorns fall at different seasons, but the clean-up work is cheerfully undertaken. We could not imagine our main tree being anything other than the typical indigenous tree of Andalucia.

On most of his courses Trent Jones was cautious about allowing an individual tree to influence shot values too greatly, since trees like all living things are mortal. But the 5th hole at Valderrama presents a glorious exception: he laid out the green so that its right-hand side is guarded by a fine cork oak, 'A bunker in the air,' as he called it, adding, 'This is probably the most unique drive and pitch hole in all of golf.' The cork in the middle of the landing area at the 2nd hole is another important tree.

VALDERRAMA

During the first five years of the Club's existence, Trent Jones and I gave enormous thought to the subject of trees; we had to, for in one way or another they impinged on almost every improvement we had in mind. Our philosophy was simple: we would protect the trees of Valderrama and they would protect our golf course from visual intrusion, as well as helping us to define the course.

If ever a particular tree had to go, we would move it if it were humanly possibly, rather than cut it down. We greatly augmented the tree population, placing them to gain privacy, enhance the fairways and focus the entrances to greens. We even planted more than 400 young corks for no other purpose than to provide a visual link between the main body of our corks and the ancient forest that adjoins the course.

The cork tree has a strong character and there are not so many species that mix in well with it. Best is the olive, a distant cousin: we have more than a thousand olive trees, although you might not notice it as the olive is smaller than the cork.

Both trees grow very slowly but the olive has the advantage that you can transplant it even when it is 200 or more years old. We have planted 600 old olive trees very successfully; notably between the 3rd and 4th; at the 7th, where they define the right-hand side of the fairway; at the 11th, 12th, 14th, and between the 14th and 15th.

While our tree operations were at their height I heard by sheer chance of a plantation of old olives near Seville that was about to be cut down to make way for a more profitable crop. I was able to save 304 of them, and because we prepared them properly before moving them to our course, the survival rate was excellent; far higher than had been predicted by the sceptics.

The arborist who guided us during these exciting times was Jim Borer of Los Angeles, a top man at the very specialised work of moving established trees from one place to another. This is an arduous process requiring not only long experience but patience, much labour, and special lifting equipment. If you are not a real tree lover, you had better not bother. But if you are, it is

VALDERRAMA

very, very rewarding. Under Borer's guidance we also brought in 80 mature pine trees for visual protection in key positions.

We have planted several thousand pines of various kinds, including some very large Mediterranean pines *(Halepensis)* that grow well and fast in our climate. These trees have been planted to screen off the golf course from the neighbouring lots that have been built up.

The visitor to Valderrama who has a keen appreciation of things visual should look around and observe how much the integrity of our golf course owes to trees planted during the last ten years. We are confident that as these trees continue to grow, Valderrama will become even more beautiful.

An 18th-century French nobleman wrote in his journal that in Spain a squirrel might run from the Pyrenees to the Mediterranean without touching the ground. Regrettably, this is no longer true, but at Valderrama the trees are safe from further depredation.

We have planted hundreds of cork oaks from a nearby nursery and have moved many more to save them from the axe.

The name Audubon inspires the various Audubon Societies, the most prestigious wildlife protection associations in the United States. The name has a ring about it even for those who do not know that John James Audubon (1785-1851) was one of the world's greatest ornithologists and wildlife illustrators. For his monumental work, *Birds of America*, he made life-size colour plates of 1065 birds.

In 1992 our Founder Member Jean Jacques (Kiko) Bemberg presented the Club with twelve prints from these original colour plates. They were immediately placed on the walls of our newly-opened snooker room, where they continue to delight the eye. I was struck by the coincidence that Kiko's gracious gift was made in the same year that the New York Audubon

This magnificent cork oak is another of Valderrama's most celebrated individual trees. It dominates the landing area in the middle of the 2nd fairway and requires that the tee shot be accurately placed to the left; or, against a strong poniente, to the right.

Society launched the USGA-Audubon Cooperative Sanctuary Program for golf courses.

Valderrama was the first European club to join the program. The goal is to inform everyone associated with golf courses about wildlife and environmental issues, and to publicly recognise golf courses that become involved in environmental projects.

To become a Certified Co-operative Sanctuary is not easy: nearly a thousand US golf courses have joined the program and only 21 have achieved full certification. Valderrama has so far obtained Certificates of Recognition in environmental planning, wildlife food enhancement and wildlife cover enhancement.

To do so we had to prepare a detailed survey of wildlife and habitats on the golf course, with recommendations for their conservation. This was done by the Club's naturalist and wildlife consultant, Martin Jacoby, MA, who is a Fellow of the Linnaean Society. His report was most encouraging, for he concluded that our golf course was already a net benefit to wildlife and

The mighty Griffon Vulture sails the air like a stately Spanish galleon.

that there were opportunities to enhance this still further.

As part of our programme we have set aside ten Sanctuaries: wild areas in the 'out of bounds' between holes which are managed for the benefit of the native wildlife in all its forms. In particular, feeding stations and nesting boxes have been provided to attract birds. Good management of the ranker vegetation allows more light for plants and better nesting conditions, and we are

VALDERRAMA

Andalucia and Morocco are the ancestral homes of the daffodil, which has spread all over the world in cultivated form. The wild species are now threatened in their native environment by human activities. Narcissus papyraceus, which fills the air with its sweet perfume, is one of the wild varieties being introduced to the Sanctuaries of Valderrama.

introducing species whose leaves will provide food for the caterpillars of rare butterflies. Bilingual plaques tell Members what may be seen in the wild parts during a round of golf, although it may be surmised that some of our less straight-hitting Members are already not uninformed.

The Sanctuary areas also provide an ideal habitat for numerous self-seeded wild flowers of the region, including daisies, gorse, autumn snowflakes, squill and various members of the rockrose family. In co-operation with local botanists and environmental agencies we are collecting and raising seed of Andalucia's various native daffodils, whose survival elsewhere is threatened by development. Our aim is to preserve them and multiply stocks and ultimately to re-introduce them to the wild.

During the preparation of his wildlife survey our naturalist recorded the sighting of no fewer than 78 species of birds, 11 mammals, four reptiles, three amphibians, 20 butterflies and three dragonflies. These are named in Appendix II.

One of the objects of the program is to raise

VALDERRAMA

No wonder the little girl is hiding: Valderrama's 'own' eagle owl must have seemed enormous. The magnificent bird can attain a wing span of 180 cm. (six feet) and is a major nocturnal predator. The species once occupied all types of country in lowland Europe but is now found only among inaccessible rocks and marshes. Eagle owls are non-migratory and strongly territorial, the males declaring their property with a characteristic deep booming call that can carry for up to 4 km.

our Members' awareness of wildlife, but in one notable episode the wildlife itself took the initiative in this process: an eagle owl, an enormous bird, was discovered wandering disconsolately on the 5th fairway. It was found to be injured, and was immediately well taken care of. 'Another has been seen in the hills nearby,' Jacoby told me, 'so perhaps there is a pair of them.' We are hopeful that in the undisturbed habitat of our Sanctuaries a pair may decide to set up home in a specially made cork-covered hut high in an oak tree.

Valderrama's location near the Strait of Gibraltar means that we are privileged to witness one of the great spectacles of the natural world. Each year in spring and autumn hundreds of thousands of migrating birds over-fly us to cross the Strait at its narrowest point between Algeciras and Tarifa. Three of the species form particularly big flocks: white storks, black kites and honey buzzards. Raptors ranging in size all the way from the sparrowhawk to the griffin vulture, 280 cm from wingtip to wingtip, can be seen travelling

One of the five carnivorous mammals to find a haven at Valderrama is the mongoose. It is up to a metre long, with a low-slung grizzled grey body, pointed muzzle and small eyes and ears. It is strictly carnivorous, though eating quite a lot of insects and worms, and is more active by day than by night. Members out for an early round may spot its distinctive tracks in dew or in bunkers.

VALDERRAMA

singly or in small groups. The smaller migrating birds often make use of our Sanctuaries to feed and rest.

Concern for the environment is much better organised these days. As a member of the USGA Environmental and Turfgrass Research Committee I was pleased when the R & A set up an advisory group under Tim Taylor to collate and disseminate information and avoid duplication. I am chairman of the group's ecology unit, and I also represent Spain on the European Golf Association's ecology unit.

A different aspect of our Club's environmental concerns is that we attach great importance to a harmonious relationship with the indigenous community, which as it happens largely constitutes our workforce. We were therefore delighted, about the time I took over full ownership of the Club in 1989, to have an opportunity to strengthen the relationship further by participating in a most worthy project.

Large flocks of migrating honey buzzards pass over Valderrama in spring and autumn.

Our workers live mainly in the nearby village of Guadiaro. In the early days we used to let them play on our course whenever possible but it came as no surprise that this golf-conscious community should dream of creating a course of its own. This was a big hill to climb, but fortunately the municipal authorities were well disposed and they responded sympathetically when an approach was made.

A committee of residents under the presidency of Sebastian Sarria, who at that time was the dining-room manager at Valderrama, put forward a proposal for a partnership deal with the council. If the council would provide the land, the committee would undertake to build initially a 9-hole course and run it as a municipal golf course. The deal was accepted and I was approached for advice and assistance. I spoke first with Robert Trent Jones, who happened to be

The rockrose family evolved in Andalucia, which is why we have so many species, some found only here. All have yellow centres surrounded by delicate papery petals of bright yellow, shocking pink or white, like the sage-leaved cistus shown here.

VALDERRAMA

The bee eater is perhaps the most beautiful of the birds of Valderrama. It is a summer visitor that can be seen every day over the course, though often high up.

my house guest at the time and he immediately visited the site. After viewing the scenic piece of land, he offered to prepare a plan for the course without fee for the local people that he had come to admire and appreciate.

Most golf-course architects would probably have drawn up plans for a fairly basic course, assuming (rightly) that the construction budget would be extremely limited and that in any case a basic layout would serve the purposes of a small rural community. Trent Jones felt otherwise: he thought that to fob off the workers of Valderrama with such a course would be patronising. The dramatic contouring of the hill-top site, with its precipitous gorge, engaged his imagination and he had no intention of doing less than justice to it. He produced a plan for nine holes worthy to grace a championship, complete with lakes and even a waterfall.

The Trent Jones design would test the villagers' construction skills to the limit, but it also inspired them. Having been given a plan for a course of the highest quality, they determined to realise it

with construction standards to match, no matter how long it took. We were able to help, not just by financial contributions but by donating, along with Toro, the equipment company, a complete irrigation system that we were replacing. In the event it was 1991 before the villagers stood proudly around the first tee and invited the mayor of San Roque to name their golf club La Cañada. The ceremony was attended also by the presidents of the Royal Spanish Golf Federation and the Andalucian Golf Federation. Juan Quiros, Manuel Pinero and Juan Franco played an exhibition match. For a country that still has far too few municipal courses, this was a landmark occasion. I was very gratified when the Club named me its first Honorary Member.

*La Cañada golf course was constructed by the villagers of Guadiaro using their own skills to a design of Robert Trent Jones.
It is probably the finest public golf course in Spain.*

Jaime Ortiz-Patiño, Sir Ian MacLaurin and James Stewart in relaxed and hopeful mood with the relief model of Valderrama golf course which was the eye-catching centrepiece of the Club's final presentation to the Ryder Cup Committee at the Berkeley Hotel, London.

THE 1997 RYDER CUP MATCH

When someone asked me at a cocktail party why I wanted to host the Ryder Cup at Valderrama I was momentarily at a loss for a reply. It was like asking a serious actor why he wanted to play Hamlet. How could any golf course superintendent not want his course to be the venue for the world's greatest golf contest?

It was not until 1993 that the Ryder Cup committee confirmed that the 1997 match would be played in Spain in recognition of the contribution Spanish players had made since Europe was first included in 1979. But the decision had been expected and I was ready. Time spent on reconnaissance is never wasted and I had carefully studied the logistics and administration of the 1991 match at Kiawah Island, South Carolina, where I had acted as an official observer for the European team. I confided my wild dream to two very good friends, members of Valderrama. It was a wise move. The two proved indispensable in preparing Valderrama's submission to host the 1997 match, and they are now equally involved in mounting the match itself.

Sir Ian MacLaurin, a member of the Board of Governors of the Club and chairman of Tesco, the leading UK supermarket chain, allies a very keen mind to a wealth of business experience and he is also an important figure in the sporting fraternity. Sir Ian and I had been at the 1989 match at The Belfry, so were already fairly conversant with the scale and scope of the organisational problems by the time we arrived at Kiawah. We returned to Spain equipped with an extensive data bank and with many ideas for our formal submission to the Ryder Cup committee.

My other confidant was James Stewart, at that time chief executive of my property group, Valderrama Estates SA. He is now the Club's general manager.

The match in Europe had never been played outside England, except once in Scotland, and the problems of staging it in Spain had to be very thoroughly examined. For a start, how many spectators could be comfortably accommodated? We had plenty of experience of galleries at the annual Volvo Masters tournaments but we had

never had a crowd remotely comparable in size to what a Ryder Cup would produce.

After planning for sixteen grandstands to hold nearly 11,000 static spectators we reckoned that we could take up to 30,000 people, including all the staff and helpers. Were there enough hotel rooms for such a number? Was there easy access by air and road? Did we have enough land for the many space-hungry amenities such as hospitality centres, exhibition tent, restaurants and refreshment tents, parking space, TV compounds and press-room space and electronic facilities for 1,200 print and broadcasting journalists? Could the road access handle the expected volume of traffic? These were just the basic questions. In addition there was a myriad of smaller but equally vital ones such as the need for first-aid centres, helicopter ambulances, on-course paramedics, a state-of-the-art communications network to provide instant scores, a rigorous security requirement, and so on.

We identified each area where we felt the Club could be deficient and we let nothing stand in the way of devising a solution. For instance, we did not have enough spare land alongside the golf course for a catering complex big enough to feed a capacity crowd, plus the thousands of workers and volunteers. So we immediately put in hand a programme for reclaiming a steep slope alongside the seventh hole by bringing in many thousand tons of fill to create a level, five-acre meadow.

It was clear that the existing coastal highway, with only one lane each way, would not provide a free flow for the expected traffic. Before we could make our submission I had to get an assurance that by the autumn of 1997 the highway would be suitably upgraded. The authorities took the problem thoroughly on board and assured us that we would have two lanes each way, a satisfactory solution even though one particular stretch of road will not be dualled in time.

When it is, before the turn of the century, the Costa del Sol will have a dual carriageway link all the way from Copenhagen to the entrance of Valderrama and on to Algeciras, Spain's main

CÓRDOBA

Jaén

Écija

SEVILLA

Lucena

El Arahal

GUADALQUIVIR

Utrera

Estepa

Río Guadaira

A N D A L U C I A

Antequera

GRANADA

Jerez

Ronda

MÁLAGA

CÁDIZ

Ubrique

Torremolinos

Marbella

Benalmádena

Motril

Jimena

Estepona

Fuengirola

Manilva

VALDERRAMA

Los Barrios

Sotogrande

San Roque

La Línea

Gibraltar

Tarifa

Algeciras

	Dual carriageway
	Under construction
	Single carriageway
	Minor roads

container port at the junction of the Atlantic and the Mediterranean.

Eventually we were satisfied that we could meet the most stringent conditions for holding the match. Further, we could offer what no other golf club in Spain could equal: a team of administrators seasoned from years of organising the Volvo Masters, with the proven expertise and experience to handle a major golf event.

By the spring of 1992 we were ready with detailed site plans and all our arrangements were in place. A press conference was called for the Tuesday after Easter at Claridge's Hotel and Sir Ian made the public announcement that Valderrama's hat was well and truly in the ring as a contender for the 1997 match. The formal presentation document and feasibility study were then handed to Neil Coles and Phil Weaver, co-chairmen of the Ryder Cup committee.

Until the Ryder Cup committee officially decided – in May 1993, 13 months after our presentation – that the 1997 event would be played in Spain, we were the only club to make a bid. After the announcement, there began a period of phony war. Other clubs put in bids, some more realistic than others. Club de Campo in Madrid and the nearby La Moraleja were well supported by those who believed that the match should be held near the nation's capital city, but autumn is convention time in Madrid and hotels are booked solid for years ahead; moreover, Turespaña – the national tourist authority, and sponsor of four PGA European Tour events each year – were against Madrid. As befitted a government agency, Turespaña took an overall national view and they maintained that the Ryder Cup should come to a Spanish tourist area and not a major city. Turespaña were well aware of the immense benefits that staging the Ryder Cup would bring to tourism.

The phony war developed into trench warfare. La Manga loomed as a serious rival to Valderrama, as it had good facilities, while if golfing values alone were to be the criterion, the superb El Saler course near Valencia would be the one we all had to fear. But what really put the cat among the

pigeons was when Tony Jacklin resigned from the Ryder Cup committee and Severiano Ballesteros was invited to fill the vacancy. Some observers thought this was a questionable move. Seve does not owe his success to going easy on the other fellow: he is one of the most competitive persons the rivalrous world of golf has ever known. It was to be expected that he would do everything he could to win the Ryder Cup for the course of his choice, and that is precisely what happened: he made no pretence of sitting in objective judgment on the other short-listed candidates. Seve had failed to get the needed backing for a new course near Madrid, where he had hoped to stage the event, and now the apple of his eye was Novo Sancti Petri, a new development along the coast from Cadiz, which had been planned by his own design company. And this was the golf course he plugged.

Sir Ian MacLaurin hands Valderrama's formal offer to stage the 1997 Ryder Cup match to Philip Weaver, co-chairman of the Ryder Cup committee, at the Club's public presentation at Claridge's Hotel, London in 1992.

Following the Club's submission, the Ryder Cup committee visited Valderrama en bloc. I showed them what we had to offer and they in turn made known their views as to what was required of a Ryder Cup course.

In January 1994 when the committee met in London to consider the formal submissions, Seve made his pitch in favour of Novo Sancti Petri and then left the meeting. He and I did not meet again until the Ryder Cup committee's press conference at Wentworth four months later. The committee named Valderrama as its choice, and as we left the meeting Seve showed his largeness of spirit: he shook me by the hand and said in free translation, 'You are too tough a nut for me!'

I am delighted that Seve and I are friends again and I look forward to working with him, as player or captain of the European team, in making the 1997 match a success. Seve's principal motive in waging his hard-fought campaign was the unshakable belief that Spain is worthy of the historic honour of acting as host to the event.

With Valderrama now 'in the frame' I assumed in my innocence that we would be able to go full steam ahead with the million and one things that had to be done. Questions needing urgent answers came tumbling over each other in my mind. Would we be responsible for planning the grandstands? If so, would it be our task to give instructions to a contractor? Would we ourselves pay the contractor? Would we be responsible for selling the tickets and, if so, would we retain a proportion of the revenue to defray our costs? Who does what? Who pays what? Who keeps what? Our requests for clarification were not met with the urgency we should have preferred.

Next to television, corporate hospitality is the lifeblood of the Ryder Cup. Already, in 1994, we were getting plenty of enquiries but even by the summer of 1995 we were still having to tell our corporate friends that we were in the dark. And this at a time when The Country Club, Brookline, Massachusetts was already busy selling corporate hospitality amenities for 1999!

Clearly, the Ryder Cup committee, accustomed to operating in the UK, faced an entirely new challenge in running the event in Spain. For example, how long would it take to arrange for a thousand telephone lines to be laid on at a remote Spanish golf club. You start that exercise, I might add, by patiently explaining to

VALDERRAMA

the responsible authority that golf is a game. That information by itself does not galvanise the authority into urgent activity, I can tell you, but it is a start.

In a way it was flattering to think that the Ryder Cup committee was so confident that we could solve all the problems, but I would have preferred to have a longer lead time. Also, I wanted to be able to develop ideas that might help the committee.

Between us, Sir Ian MacLaurin, James Stewart and I have had a fair bit of entrepreneurial experience and we were eager to exploit it. For example, it should be axiomatic that the host organisers of a major sporting event be given confidential notice so that they can block off hotel rooms as necessary before the public announcement is made. This was not done, and the best we could achieve was to enter into agreements with eleven of the largest hotels, using an ingenious system pioneered at the 1994 soccer World Cup in America.

This is how it works. Say you make a booking for seven nights at the Hotel Splendide: Valderrama and the hotel would put your money into a special account and give you seven envelopes, each dated for one night of your week's stay. Inside each envelope is a cheque for the amount of one night's stay, in itself a fair guarantee that the hotel will keep your room open for you. But if, say, a dishonest night porter should take a bribe and let your room to someone else, then the hotel will forfeit three times the room rate from its deposit in the bank account. Now that really *is* a guarantee that your room will be kept for you. I might add that the rates negotiated are in every case lower than the regular tariff. Another big advantage is that if by chance you have to leave early you can transfer to a friend or business associate your unexpired envelopes in the sure knowledge that the room will be available to the bearer of the envelope.

The Ryder Cup committee may have thought that in floating this and other ideas I was stepping outside my proper role. In our defence I and my associates can point to proven track records in the

The moment all of us at Valderrama had been waiting for: the 1994 announcement by Ken Schofield on behalf of the Ryder Cup committee that our club had been selected for the signal honour of staging the match.

many activities we have undertaken. We also have the best possible world-wide contacts and could also provide any needed risk capital to make our ideas work. This can be very helpful when the official bodies have limited resources, as was the case here.

Frustrating though our early experiences may have been, it all ended amicably when, early in June 1995, a venue agreement that satisfied both parties was signed. Sir Ian MacLaurin, Ramon Davila who is our Club Secretary and legal counsel, James Stewart and I were pleased with this outcome. We felt that we had been allocated a fair share of the action and had been given scope to exercise our energies. But in any case nothing would have affected our determination to carry Europe's – and Spain's – banner with honour and in so doing to make Valderrama the best-presented venue in the history of the Ryder Cup.

At last we were able to make firm plans, with 27 months still in hand; not quite as much, it is true, as our friends at The Country Club,

Brookline, Massachusetts, who had been given 52 months to prepare for the 1999 Ryder Cup.

The transformation of the Ryder Cup from a low-key encounter to one with a TV audience in the hundreds of millions makes a fascinating story. The intention of Samuel Ryder, the successful English seed merchant who donated the famous gold chalice, was simply to foster a friendly relationship between the professional golfers of America and the British Isles. Camaraderie was to be of greater importance than the result.

Quite quickly after the inaugural match in 1927, the Americans achieved such dominance that the match held virtually no public interest in the United States. It was more of an exhibition than a sporting contest and its significance to the American players was that it offered the one opportunity for them to be selected for the honour of representing their country. A Ryder Cup blazer was highly prized as the sporting equivalent of a medal of honour. In Britain and Ireland the attitude could hardly have been more different. Players and public alike saw the matches as the

VALDERRAMA

'I enjoyed my day of golf on your superb course,' wrote President George Bush after playing Valderrama in August 1993 with his wife Barbara and the Club president. He later added, 'I'll be back for the Ryder Cup if it's humanly possible.'

pinnacle of sporting contests, the match-play equivalent of the Open championship itself. If it had overtones of David and Goliath, this served to heighten the interest on those rare occasions when the mighty Goliath was humbled.

Jack Nicklaus was an enthusiastic supporter of the Ryder Cup tradition and he suggested that it would be a more even-handed contest if recruitment for the Great Britain and Ireland team were extended to continental Europe, where stars such as Severiano Ballesteros, Antonio Garrido, José-Maria Canizares, Manuel Pinero and Bernhard Langer were emerging. And indeed, the inclusion of Europe in 1979 brought about a magical transformation. U.S. dominance was truly challenged for the first time in nearly half a century, and in 1983 at the PGA National course in Florida the Americans were heartily relieved to come away with a one-point victory from the last match of the series. Two years later, at The Belfry, Europe triumphed convincingly and America awoke to the fact that it was involved in a major sporting contest.

'One swallow does not make a summer,' the Americans may have thought, but a greater sensation was to follow. In 1987, captained by the greatest player of the game, Jack Nicklaus, and on his very own course at Muirfield Village, Ohio, the Americans were beaten for the first time on their own soil. From now on there would be no more easy touches; the Ryder Cup was a fierce battle for national pride and a major international sporting occasion, of the stature of Wimbledon, the soccer World Cup and the Olympic Games.

I end this memoir of Valderrama's first ten years with some speculations about the 1997 Ryder Cup. Unless something totally unforeseen occurs, Valderrama will be in as good a condition as any previous Ryder Cup course. Its narrow fairways, punishing roughs and slick greens might be thought to favour the Americans, but I myself think differently. Europe's team seems likely to consist largely of players – their names can be read in my chapter on the Volvo Masters – who have had very thorough experience of the course

and its two prevailing winds. This experience could be a key factor in the outcome.

I write without knowledge of the 1995 result, but I am convinced that even if, at Oak Hill, the U.S. assert their former mastery, they will have a battle of giants on their hands when they come to Valderrama.

And how will I present the course? Simple: exactly as the Ryder Cup committee asks me to. It is their responsibility. I know how it would be set up if I were in charge – and it would be the same way that I set it up for the Volvo Masters, which I consider suits the course best – but luckily this burden is not mine.

Whoever wins the 1997 event, our golf course will come under more intense scrutiny than ever before and I welcome this. If there are any lessons to be learned, we will use them to make Valderrama an even better course than it is already.

A dewy morning reflects the sun on the 2nd fairway.

VALDERRAMA

THE ROBERT TRENT JONES DESIGN PHILOSOPHY

In late 1960, I was engaged to design a golf course, which was called the New course at first, then Las Aves: later, after my friend Jaime Ortiz-Patiño purchased the course from Financiera Sotogrande SA, he renamed it Valderrama.

I was already familiar with the countryside and the weather pattern from my experience in building the Old Course. I was therefore able to go straight into my usual design routine, making myself thoroughly familiar with the property and concentrating in particular on identifying attractive sites for greens. It may sound like putting the cart before the horse, but golf courses are better designed backwards in this manner. Having envisioned how a green will fit naturally into its position, I can visualise the most suitable type of shot that must be played into it. This in turn suggests the appropriate length of the hole.

Of course, many other considerations of a technical nature must be reconciled in this equation, such as drainage, ease of maintenance, irrigation, playability for every category of golfer, fairness and balance, free circulation of air, light and above all, safety, both of other players and of people and property outside the course boundaries. Every decision therefore has to be subjected to a long check list of imperatives.

When an architect is given a flat, unprepossessing site he has no alternative but to think in terms of moving substantial quantities of earth. For one thing, he will need excavated materials to build up tees and greens. Besides, the resulting lakes and mounds will add greatly to the visual and playing interest of the course. On beautiful, undulating land such as I was fortunate enough to find at Valderrama all my instincts are to leave well enough alone, so far as this is possible. After all, Nature has spent many millenia shaping this piece of land and Nature is the best golf-course architect. The task of the human designer is to identify the course which is already waiting to be discovered. Obviously, a certain amount of minor adjustment will be needed because of golfing considerations, but I prefer to keep this to the minimum and to take great pains to respect the integrity of the landscape.

VALDERRAMA

This last point applies most strongly in respect of trees. A mature tree may have taken 400 years to reach its noble stature but it can be felled in minutes. My policy is therefore to leave trees for as long as possible during the construction process. After all, second thoughts may result in a change in the routing of a hole. So, when New Sotogrande was nearly complete, some of the fairways were still furnished with mature trees waiting on death row as it were. I pointed these out to Joe McMicking as we toured the course, explaining that the time had now come for their sentences to be carried out. 'Leave them be,' he commanded. I questioned this: on what basis could we validly allow them to remain obstructing the fairways? 'It is the golden rule,' Joe replied. 'What golden rule is that?,' I inquired, thinking he might be referring to some tree preservation order imposed by the municipal authorities. He replied: 'I have the gold; I make the rules.'

But although I thoroughly shared his detestation of destroying trees, I reluctantly had to insist on removing some of them for the sake of playability. In defence of my vandalism, I may add that over the years we have saved many hundreds of mature trees that had been condemned to the axe by others and that we were able to bring to Valderrama at great expense and transplant. Those wonderfully gnarled olives near the 7th fairway and on the 11th, for instance, are more than 400 years old and were brought all the way from Seville.

Some people claim that they can recognise a Robert Trent Jones golf course by some personal trademark, or in some ill-defined intention to humiliate the great players. I strongly object to the charge. In design detail I shape bunkers, for example, to fit the topography and locate them to play specific roles in the strategic purpose of the hole. I repeat myself in only one respect, and this is to impose the same abstract value on every hole of every course I have ever designed. This is to make the hole hard for a good player to gain his par but easy to make bogey. If there is a Robert Trent Jones trademark it is this philosophy of

VALDERRAMA

hard par, easy bogey. To call this 'a Robert Trent Jonesism' is really rather silly, because most architects work to this principle. Nevertheless, I was guided in my design of Valderrama by this ideal of hard par, easy bogey; hence the severe contouring of some of the greens. Newcomers to Valderrama frequently remark that they find the greens difficult to read, and some have been heard shamefacedly to admit to having played an intended uphill putt on what turned out to be a downslope. Much as I would enjoy receiving credit for having contrived these optical illusions, I have to admit that they arise mainly by happy chance. There are however some tricks the architect can exploit. The road behind the 13th and 15th greens, both notoriously difficult to putt, is slightly uphill and this may create a false horizon that may contradict the signals from the human gyroscope of the inner ear. But most optical illusions are a matter of luck.

The last, and very important, factor that influenced my planning of Valderrama was the wind. Generally, the architect makes provision for one prevailing wind. On this coastline there are two: the offshore poniente, hot and dehydrating in summer after crossing Spain's arid central savannah but with a biting edge in winter from the snow-capped Medina-Sidonia sierras, and the humid, onshore levante. Both had to be taken into consideration and both contribute to the ideal that a course should provide a test for every club in the bag and every stroke in the player's repertoire. But course design and playing strategy can only be discussed in the context of still conditions. That means generalising without reference to the variable factors of weather and underfoot conditions. At least at Valderrama there is precious little variation in underfoot conditions because the greens and fairways are maintained to a uniform standard of excellence all the year round. So join me now on a brief tour of the course.

VALDERRAMA

HOLE 1.

This is a fairly conventional opening hole since it makes no serious demands on the golfer, at least in excessive length, although it does demand extreme accuracy. It is an opportunity to limber up the muscles and concentrate the mind for the real challenge ahead.

HOLE 2.

That tree in the middle of the fairway has probably been the subject of more verbal abuse than any other natural feature on the course. It is more sinned against than sinning because it performs a valuable function. Take aim on that tree and shape your drive with a shade of draw and you will finish in the perfect spot for your approach to the green.

HOLE 3.

From the elevated tee the hole plays about half a club shorter than its actual length. The dangers, although severe, are plain to see and the green is a generous-sized target for this length of shot.

HOLE 4.

This is generally regarded as Valderrama's signature hole, whatever that means. A good drive and second shot favouring the right-hand side will finish in the ideal spot for an approach shot to the green.

HOLE 5.

Do not be deceived by the widest fairway on the course. This is an accuracy hole, calling for precise placement of the tee shot, usually with an iron, to line up your pitch with the narrow entrance to the small green. A tree – my 'bunker in the sky' – threatens a shot from the right side of the fairway.

HOLE 6.

This is a massive green for a modestly sized par-three but the target area is restricted if you are going to leave yourself with the desired uphill putt, depending upon the siting of the cup.

VALDERRAMA

HOLE 7.
This hole has gone through several changes of character, at one time being a par-five which the pros played as a par-four, then becoming a par-four for the Members who mainly played it as a par-five. It is now a formidable par-four for everyone.

HOLE 8.
In the strategic sense this is the same challenge as the 5th, but on a slightly reduced scale. First you have to identify the precise area on the generous fairway that will give you the optimum line through the guardian trees for your pitch. An iron from the tee is usually the sensible choice.

HOLE 9.
Originally this was the 18th, so the standards are demanding, commensurate with a closing hole. A long second must be played through a narrow chute of trees to a heavily defended green.

HOLE 10.
Now the screw really begins to tighten because the second half demands slightly higher standards of accuracy and shot making, particularly in controlling fades and draws. A touch of fade off the tee will leave your ball dry and in position for a pitch shot to the elevated green.

HOLE 11.
When into the levante, this is a genuine par-five. The best line is to play up the left side of the sloping fairway or, at least, to make sure your ball is up on the left after your second shot so that you get a clear sight of the green for your pitch.

HOLE 12.
As you stand on the tee you might assume this to be the hardest par-three on the course. Actually, that pleasure is yet to come. A high, fading tee shot is usually the preferred tactic.

VALDERRAMA

HOLE 13.

Accuracy rather than length off the tee is demanded here. The trees on either side of the narrow fairway are not thick but it is still a lottery if you hit in among them. This green in particular bears very close study before you decide on the line and speed.

HOLE 14.

There is a slight kink in this fairway. From the tee it may appear that the best line is along the trees on the right but actually the preferred angle for the approach to the elevated green is from the left side.

HOLE 15.

This is the start of what is designed to be a strong finish to end the round. The tee shot will normally need your longest iron, or a wood. Hitting this long, narrow green is less than half the battle. The contours of the green are severe and most deceptive.

HOLE 16.

Here again, in the manner of the 14th, only half the fairway, the left side, is the effective playing area. It is one of the keys to the understanding of Valderrama that the straight holes are best played as slight dog-legs. The trick is determining the optimum target areas, according to the varying conditions.

HOLE 17.

For years this hole was enormously long and not much else. The green was unreachable in two strokes, except in abnormal conditions, so the only requirement of the first two strokes was to move forward. By shortening the hole and creating a lake in front of the green, the hole has become visually much more attractive, much more exciting for spectators, and tactically much more demanding on the players. Now the agonising decision must be made: to lay up short of the water, or go for the carry and the sure reward of a birdie.

VALDERRAMA

HOLE 18.

Here the tee shot is paramount. The drive under and through a chute of trees can run through the fairway into more trees unless the shot is drawn to a precise degree, a high-risk play calling for abundant confidence and skill. Prudence may demand an iron off the tee, but that will leave an inordinately long second to the tightly trapped green.

LAST WORD

When you have played Valderrama I hope you will understand and appreciate how the principle of easy bogey, hard par enhances the satisfaction of golf. It is commonplace in golf clubs for the members grossly to overvalue the quality of their courses, a very natural and harmless conceit. But when a competition comes along this false pride sometimes gives rise to a determination that 'they won't make a fool of our course.' And so the course is tricked up to a degree that makes fools of those who prepared it. That never happens at Valderrama. Indeed, the reverse is the case. No effort or expense is spared to get the greens absolutely true and to present the fairways in condition to delight the most fastidious of shot makers. Low scores are possible and are welcomed as both the hard-won rewards for brilliant golf and as a compliment to the green staff. That is exactly the way things should be and it illustrates another of the principles that I have always adopted in my approach to design: golf should be a pleasure, not a penance.

Robert Trent Jones

VALDERRAMA

VALDERRAMA

WILDLIFE RECORDED AT VALDERRAMA GOLF CLUB 1993-4

Birds

(numbers refer to pages in *The Birds of Britain & Europe with North Africa & the Middle East* by Heinzel, Fitter & Parslow, Collins 1987)

Grey Heron [Garza] *Ardea cinerea* 35
Cattle Egret [Garcilla bueyera] *Bubulcus ibis* 37
White Stork [Cigüena] *Ciconia ciconia* 43
Mallard [Ánade real] *Anas platyrhynchos* 53
Osprey [Águila pescadora] *Pandion haliætus* 71
Black Kite [Milano negro] *Milvus migrans* 73
Buzzard [Ratonero común] *Buteo buteo* 77
Honey Buzzard [Halcón abejero] *Pernis apivorus* 77
Booted Eagle [Águila calzada] *Hieraætus pennatus* 79
Kestrel [Cernícalo vulgar] *Falco tinnunculus* 95
Red-legged Partridge [Perdix roja] *Alectoris rufa* 103
Moorhen [Polla de agua] *Gallinula chloropus* 117
Common Sandpiper [Andarríos chico]
 Actitis hypoleucos 133
Wood Pigeon [Paloma torcaz] *Columba palumbus* 171
Turtle Dove [Tórtola] *Streptopelia turtur* 173
Cuckoo [Cuco] *Cuculus canorus* 175
Barn Owl [Lechuza] *Tyto alba* 177
Eagle Owl [Buho real] *Bubo bubo* 177
Scops Owl [Autillo] *Otus scops* 179
Little Owl [Mochuelo] *Athene noctua* 181
Red-necked Nightjar [Chotocabras pardo]
 Caprimulgus ruficollis 185
Pallid Swift [Vencejo pálido] *Apus pallidus* 187

Swift [Vencejo común] *Apus apus* 187
White-rumped Swift [Vencejo culiblanco] *Apus caffer* 187
Bee-eater [Abejaruco] *Merops apiaster* 189
Hoopoe [Abubilla] *Upupa epops* 191
Green Woodpecker [Pico] *Picus viridis* 193
Great Spotted Woodpecker [Picapuertas]
 Dendrocopus major 195
Wryneck [Torcecuello] *Jynx torquilla* 197
Crested Lark [Cogujada común] *Galerida cristata* 205
Wood Lark [Totovia] *Lullula arborea* 205
House Martin [Avión común] *Delichon urbica* 207
Red-rumped Swallow [Golondrina daurica]
 Hirundo daurica 207
Swallow [Golondrina común] *Hirundo rustica* 207
Meadow Pipit [Bisbita común] *Anthus pratensis* 209
Red-throated Pipit [Bisbita campestre]
 Anthus cervinus 209
Tree Pipit [Bisbita arbórea] *Anthus trivialis* 209
Grey Wagtail [Lavandera cascadeña]
 Motacilla cinerea 213
White Wagtail [Lavandera blanca] *Motacilla alba* 213
Yellow Wagtail [Lavandera buyera] *Motacilla flava* 215
Woodchat Shrike [Alcaudón común]
 Lanius senator 219
Blackcap [Curruca capirotada] *Sylvia atricapilla* 223
Cetti's Warbler [Ruisenor bastardo] *Cettia cettia* 227
Olivaceous Warbler [Zarcero pálido]
 Hippolais pallida 229

VALDERRAMA

Whitethroat [Curruca zarcera] *Sylvia communis* 230
Sardinian Warbler [Curruca cabecinegra]
  Sylvia melanocephala 233
Dartford Warbler [Curruca rabilarga] *Sylvia undata* 235
Chiffchaff [Mosquitero común]
  Phylloscopus collybita 237
Willow Warbler [Mosquitero musical]
  Phylloscopus trochilus 237
Firecrest [Reyezuelo] *Regulus ignicapillus* 239
Pied Flycatcher [Papamoscas cerrojillo]
  Ficedula hypoleuca 241
Spotted Flycatcher [Papamoscas gris]
  Muscicapa striata 241
Stonechat [Tarabilla común] *Saxicola torquata* 243
Whinchat [Tarabilla norteña] *Saxicola rubetra* 243
Black Redstart [Colirrojo tizón]
  Phoenicurus ochrurus 251
Redstart [Colirrojo real] *Phoenicurus phoenicurus* 251
Robin [Petirrojo] *Erithracus rubecula* 253
Nightingale [Ruiseñor] *Luscinia megarhynchos* 255
Blackbird [Mirlo] *Turdus merula* 257
Mistle Thrush [Zorzal charlo] *Turdus viscivorus* 259
Song Thrush [Zorzal común] *Turdus philomelos* 259
Blue Tit [Herrerillo común] *Parus cæruleus* 267
Great Tit [Carbonero mayor] *Parus major* 267
Short-toed Treecreeper [Agateador]
  Certhia brachydactyla 273
Wren [Chóchin] *Troglodytes troglodytes* 273

Corn Bunting [Triguero] *Miliaria calandra* 275
Cirl Bunting [Escribano soteño] *Emberiza cirlus* 277
Chaffinch [Pinzón común] *Fringilla coelebs* 285
Goldfinch [Jilguero] *Carduelis carduelis* 287
Greenfinch [Verderón común] *Carduelis chloris* 287
Hawfinch [Picogordo] *Coccothraustes coccothraustes* 289
Linnet [Pardillo común] *Carduelis cannabina* 291
Serin [Verdecillo] *Serinus serinus* 293
Crossbill [Piquituerto] *Loxia curvirostra* 296
House Sparrow [Gorrión común] *Passer domesticus* 299
Spotless Starling [Estornino negro] *Sturnus unicolor* 303
Jay [Arrendajo] *Garrulus glandarius* 305
Jackdaw [Grajilla] *Corvus monedula* 311
Mammals
(numbers refer to plates in *Mammals of Britain &
Europe* by Macdonald & Barrett, Collins 1993)
Western Hedgehog [Erizo] *Erinaceus europæus* 2
Blind Mole [Topo] *Talpa cæca* 7
Fox [Zorro] *Vulpes vulpes* 18
Badger [Tejón] *Meles meles* 21
Otter [Nutria] *Lutra lutra* 22
Weasel [Comandreja] *Mustela nivalis* 25
Genet [Geneta] *Genetta genetta* 27
Mongoose [Meloncillo] *Herpestes ichneumon* 27
Wood Mouse [Ratón silvestre] *Apodemus sylvaticus* 52
Mediterranean Pine Vole [Topillo]
  Pitymys duodecimcostatus 60
Rabbit [Conejo] *Oryctolagus cuniculus* 64

VALDERRAMA

Reptiles

(numbers refer to page of plate in *A Field Guide to the Reptiles & Amphibians of Britain & Europe* by Arnold & Burton, Collins 1978)

Large Psammodromus [Largatija colilarga] *Psammodromus algirus* 116

Ocelated Lizard [Largato ocelado] *Lacerta lepida* 125

Iberian Wall Lizard [Largatija ibérica]
  Podarcis hispanica 142

Southern Smooth Snake [Culebra lisa meridional]
  Coronella girondica 205

Amphibians

(numbers refer to page of plate in *A Field Guide to the Reptiles & Amphibians of Britain & Europe* by Arnold & Burton, Collins 1978)

Stripeless Tree Frog [Ranita] *Hyla meridionalis* 68

Painted Frog [Sapillo pintojo] *Discoglossus pictus* 49

Iberian Green Frog [Rana verde] *Rana perezei* (not described by Arnold but see page 84 for difficulty)

Butterflies

(numbers refer to pages in *A Field Guide to the Butterflies of Britain & Europe* by Higgins & Hargreaves, Collins 1983)

Spanish Festoon [Arlequin] *Zerynthia rumina* 27

Large White [Blanc de la col] *Pieris brassicae* 31

Small White [Blanquita de la col] *Artogeia rapae* 33

Green-striped White [Blanc verderrayada]
  Euchloe belemia 39

Freyer's Dappled White *Euchloe crameri*
  (not *simplonia* as in Higgins 39)

Orangetip [Aurora] *Anthocharis cardamines* 40

Clouded Yellow [Colias común] *Colias crocea* 46

Brimstone [Limonera] *Gonepteryx rhamni* 51

Cleopatra [Cleopatra] *Gonepteryx cleopatra* 51

Wood Whte [Blanca esbelta] *Leptidea sinapis* 53

False Ilex Hairstreak [Querquera] *Nordmannia esculi* 59

Lang's Short-tailed Blue [Gris estriada]
  Syntarucus pirithous 67

Holly Blue [Náyade] *Celastrina argiolus* 71

Common Blue [Ícaro] *Polyommatus icarus* 94

Red Admiral [Vanesa atalanta] *Vanessa atalanta* 104

Painted Lady [Cardera] *Cynthia cardui* 107

Meadow Brown [Loba] *Maniola jurtina* 186

Spanish Gatekeeper [Lobito listado]
  Pyronia bathseba 190

Speckled Wood [Maculada] *Pararge ægeria* 199

Wall Brown [Saltacercas] *Lasiommata megera* 199

Dragonflies

(numbers are references in *A Field Guide to the Dragonflies of Britain, Europe & North Africa* by d'Aguilar, Dommanget & Préchac, Collins 1986)

Platycnemis acutipennis 15

Emperor Dragonfly *Anax imperator* 75

Red-veined Darter *Sympetrum fonscolombii* 113

VALDERRAMA

VOLVO MASTERS RESULTS

27th-30th October 1988   Purse £351,690

	SCORES				TOTAL		SCORES				TOTAL
Nick Faldo	74	71	71	68	284	Michael Allen	73	76	76	76	301
Severiano Ballesteros	68	72	74	72	286	David Whelan	76	74	77	74	301
Sandy Lyle	68	71	75	74	288	Mark James	73	76	75	77	301
Ian Woosnam	75	74	70	70	289	Ronan Rafferty	77	76	71	77	301
Roger Chapman	71	77	70	75	293	Vicente Fernandez	78	76	76	71	301
Eamon Darcy	74	71	74	74	293	Derrick Cooper	74	76	73	78	301
Mats Lanner	77	70	74	73	294	Gordon J. Brand	78	76	71	76	301
Anders Sorensen	76	67	76	75	294	David Gilford	77	76	74	74	301
Peter Fowler	77	71	71	75	294	Denis Durnian	73	75	75	79	302
Christy O'Connor Jr.	78	73	70	73	294	Mark McNulty	75	79	71	77	302
José-Maria Canizares	76	76	67	76	295	Eduardo Romero	79	70	77	76	302
Neil Hansen	77	72	75	71	295	Ignacio Gervas	82	71	79	71	303
Howard Clark	73	73	74	76	296	David Williams	74	76	76	77	303
Manuel Pinero	74	71	81	70	296	Richard Boxall	78	72	79	74	303
Neil Coles	78	76	72	71	297	Paul Way	74	78	76	75	303
Peter Baker	72	74	75	77	298	Ross McFarlane	79	73	80	73	305
Manuel Calero	77	73	73	75	298	Johan Rystrom	75	77	78	75	305
Ove Sellberg	71	74	76	77	298	Malcolm MacKenzie	73	80	75	77	305
José-Maria Olazabal	78	74	69	77	298	Bernard Gallacher	76	72	84	73	305
Simon Bishop	74	72	79	74	299	Jimmy Heggarty	77	76	75	77	305
Tony Charnley	74	72	75	78	299	Bill Longmuir	75	76	83	72	306
Des Smyth	73	81	71	74	299	Paul Curry	79	71	78	78	306
David J. Russell	74	79	74	73	300	Juan Anglada	75	77	76	79	307
Carl Mason	75	72	79	74	300	David Feherty	77	77	72	81	307
Barry Lane	74	75	75	76	300	David Llewellyn	73	76	78	81	307

VALDERRAMA

26th-29th October 1989　　Purse £400,000

	SCORES				TOTAL		SCORES				TOTAL
Ronan Rafferty	72	69	70	71	282	Mike Smith	72	75	77	73	297
Nick Faldo	74	68	72	69	283	Derrick Cooper	76	69	77	75	297
José-Maria Olazabal	69	70	74	74	287	Bill Longmuir	74	77	72	74	297
Sandy Lyle	70	76	69	74	289	Jean Van De Velde	74	74	75	74	297
Peter Fowler	75	72	69	74	290	David Gilford	79	73	73	73	298
Mark James	77	70	71	72	290	David Williams	75	73	76	74	298
Howard Clark	73	70	74	73	290	Manuel Pinero	74	75	73	77	299
Craig Parry	73	68	75	75	291	Mats Lanner	73	73	76	77	299
Vicente Fernandez	75	73	73	71	292	Mark Mouland	79	72	76	73	300
Eduardo Romero	73	73	74	72	292	Mike Harwood	75	72	77	76	300
Ove Sellberg	75	74	73	70	292	David Feherty	74	73	76	77	300
Andrew Murray	75	71	72	75	293	Paul Carrigill	73	77	71	79	300
Roger Chapman	73	72	77	71	293	Vijay Singh	76	72	75	77	300
Peter Senior	73	78	68	74	293	Keith Waters	75	72	80	73	300
Ian Woosnam	71	69	75	78	293	Philip Parkin	74	74	76	77	301
José-Maria Canizares	75	73	75	70	293	Andrew Sherborne	75	74	76	76	301
Tony Charnley	76	75	73	71	295	Bryan Norton	74	77	75	76	302
Mark McNulty	72	73	75	75	295	Paul Way	81	71	76	74	302
Christy O'Connor, Jr.	72	74	72	77	295	Sam Torrance	73	78	75	77	303
Luis Carbonetti	74	71	75	76	296	Emmanuel Dussart	77	74	76	76	303
Peter Teravainen	72	74	78	72	296	Bernard Gallacher	72	78	74	79	303
Richard Boxall	78	73	74	71	296	Frank Nobilo	75	75	76	78	304
Miguel Angel Martin	74	75	74	73	296	Mike Clayton	76	74	81	73	304
Brett Ogle	75	71	78	73	297	Philip Walton	81	71	78	76	306
Michael Allen	76	73	73	75	297	Miguel Angel Jiménez	78	72	80	76	306
Rick Hartmann	75	77	75	70	297						

VALDERRAMA

25th-28th October 1990   Purse £450,000

	SCORES				TOTAL		SCORES				TOTAL
Mike Harwood	70	72	73	71	286	Mark Roe	75	74	76	72	297
Sam Torrance	69	73	72	73	287	Paul Broadhurst	78	77	72	70	297
Steven Richardson	71	73	70	73	287	José-Maria Canizares	73	72	77	75	297
Bernhard Langer	72	71	72	73	288	Frank Nobilo	78	74	73	73	298
Anders Försbrand	75	69	71	73	288	David Williams	72	73	79	74	298
José-Maria Olazabal	72	69	74	73	288	James Spence	77	72	75	75	299
Mark McNulty	73	73	71	71	288	Michael McLean	74	79	73	73	299
Colin Montgomerie	71	72	71	75	289	Mike Clayton	73	73	80	73	299
David Feherty	70	77	67	75	289	Jim Rutledge	72	78	73	77	300
Rodger Davis	74	71	74	72	291	Mats Lanner	73	76	74	77	300
Tony Johnstone	74	74	74	70	292	Magnus Persson	70	80	75	77	302
Howard Clark	73	73	70	76	292	Miguel Angel Jiménez	75	74	76	77	302
Gordon Brand, Jr.	79	68	71	74	292	Malcolm Mackenzie	77	73	73	80	303
Vicente Fernandez	76	73	73	70	292	Peter Fowler	74	75	79	75	303
Rick Hartmann	74	71	75	72	292	Eduardo Romero	78	73	74	78	303
Christy O'Connor, Jr.	72	74	71	76	293	John Bland	73	76	76	79	304
José Rivero	76	65	75	77	293	Stephen McAllister	79	74	76	76	305
Grant Turner	71	77	73	72	293	Mark James	78	74	77	77	306
Miguel Angel Martin	72	73	76	72	293	Richard Boxall	75	82	72	78	307
Vijay Singh	74	74	73	72	293	Costantino Rocca	75	77	77	79	308
Sandy Lyle	73	74	75	72	294	Paul Way	79	76	75	84	314
Ian Woosnam	74	72	76	72	294	Philip Walton	78	81	75	82	316
Ove Sellberg	78	72	73	72	295	Eamonn Darcy	72	84			Withdrew
Ronan Rafferty	71	74	76	74	295	Russell Claydon	75	75			Withdrew
Mark Mouland	72	76	74	74	296	Brett Ogle	74	72			Withdrew
Des Smyth	74	72	75	75	296	Roger Chapman	74	72			Withdrew
Anders Sorensen	75	79	69	73	296	Derrick Cooper	81	76	72		Withdrew

VALDERRAMA

24th–27th October 1991   Purse £600,000

	SCORES				TOTAL		SCORES				TOTAL
Rodger Davis	68	73	68	71	280	Mike Harwood	71	72	77	73	293
Nick Faldo	72	70	71	68	281	Jean Van de Velde	72	73	74	75	294
Bernhard Langer	70	69	70	74	283	Jesper Parnevik	69	74	78	73	294
Severiano Ballesteros	72	73	69	70	284	Philip Walton	74	73	69	79	295
Steven Richardson	68	70	76	70	284	José Rivero	75	71	75	74	295
Mark James	67	72	72	73	284	David Feherty	75	74	74	72	295
Costantino Rocca	72	67	72	75	286	Michael McLean	76	70	75	74	295
Mark McNulty	71	71	74	71	287	Sam Torrance	73	75	76	71	295
Craig Parry	71	69	73	75	288	Russell Claydon	72	73	73	77	295
Sandy Lyle	71	73	73	71	288	Per-Ulrik Johansson	72	70	80	73	295
James Spence	70	74	73	71	288	David J. Russell	74	73	73	76	296
Frank Nobilo	74	65	75	75	289	Vijay Singh	74	72	78	72	296
José-Maria Olazabal	73	72	74	70	289	Tony Johnstone	70	73	79	74	296
Barry Lane	71	72	72	74	289	Gavin Levenson	77	73	74	73	297
Gordon Brand, Jr.	74	71	72	73	290	Jeff Hawkes	80	71	74	73	298
Colin Montgomerie	73	72	72	73	290	Roger Chapman	69	76	83	70	298
Mark Roe	74	70	72	75	291	Paul Way	74	78	72	75	299
David Gilford	73	73	77	68	291	Eduardo Romero	76	72	78	73	299
Keith Waters	71	70	74	76	291	Andrew Sherborne	71	75	77	76	299
Peter O'Malley	74	75	69	74	292	Carl Mason	75	75	75	75	300
Ronan Rafferty	74	70	74	74	292	Anders Försbrand	73	71	79	77	300
Vicente Fernandez	74	69	74	75	292	Miguel Angel Martin	74	76	77	74	301
Miguel Angel Jiménez	78	71	71	72	292	Mats Lanner	75	75	78	73	301
Peter Mitchell	69	73	72	78	292	Paul Broadhurst	78	77	77	69	301
Eamonn Darcy	74	70	71	78	293	Mark Davis	76	75	76	78	305
Malcolm Mackenzie	75	72	71	75	293	Peter Fowler	79	80	73	73	305
Peter Teravainen	77	72	74	70	293	Howard Clark	81	77	75	82	315

VALDERRAMA

29th October–1st November 1992   Purse £660,000

	SCORES				TOTAL
Sandy Lyle	72	70	72	73	287
Colin Montgomerie	76	70	72	69	287
(Lyle defeated Montgomerie on first extra hole.)					
Christy O'Connor Jr.	76	68	71	74	289
Eduardo Romero	74	72	70	74	290
Tony Johnstone	78	68	70	74	290
José-Maria Olazabal	75	72	73	71	291
Brett Ogle	77	72	72	70	291
Bernhard Langer	72	76	70	74	292
Gordon Brand, Jr.	70	74	76	72	292
Peter Mitchell	73	73	76	71	293
Glen Day	78	71	72	72	293
Miguel Angel Jiménez	73	72	76	72	293
Steven Richardson	71	74	78	71	294
Wayne Westner	74	71	76	73	294
Frank Nobilo	74	73	73	74	294
Ian Woosnam	76	75	74	69	294
Ian Palmer	73	78	72	72	295
Anders Försbrand	79	74	76	67	296
Mark Roe	80	71	72	73	296
Andrew Sherborne	75	71	73	78	297
Costantino Rocca	74	78	73	73	298
Ronan Rafferty	77	68	74	79	298
David Gilford	73	75	77	74	299
Robert Karlsson	77	72	73	77	299
Nick Faldo	73	79	74	73	299
Joakim Haeggman	79	74	73	73	299
Darren Clarke	73	76	76	75	300

	SCORES				TOTAL
Jamie Spence	70	75	74	81	300
Vicente Fernandez	79	75	76	70	300
José Rivero	78	73	73	76	300
Jim Payne	77	73	73	77	300
Mark James	76	74	79	72	301
Mark McNulty	76	74	74	77	301
Rodger Davis	74	76	72	79	301
Malcolm Mackenzie	77	73	73	78	301
José-Maria Canizares	74	78	76	73	301
Santiago Luna	79	74	72	76	301
David Feherty	74	70	78	79	301
Miguel Angel Martin	79	76	72	75	302
Gary Evans	75	79	77	72	303
Vijay Singh	82	73	73	75	303
Peter Baker	79	72	77	75	303
Howard Clark	77	77	79	71	304
Barry Lane	79	76	75	74	304
Mats Lanner	80	77	74	74	305
Mike McLean	73	77	79	76	305
Per-Ulrik Johansson	80	73	75	79	307
David J. Russell	86	75	73	74	308
Philip Walton	74	73	80	83	310
Peter O'Malley	79	78	78	77	312
Johan Rystrom	79	83	75	75	312
Paul Way	80	79	83	77	319
Tony Jacklin	81	83	80	76	320
Paul Broadhurst	77	84			Withdrew

VALDERRAMA

4th-7th November 1993   Purse £750,000

Name	SCORES				TOTAL	Name	SCORES				TOTAL
Colin Montgomerie	69	70	67	68	274	Eduardo Romero	70	75	73	73	291
Darren Clarke	69	73	65	68	275	Mark Roe	72	76	70	74	292
David Gilford	68	72	67	69	276	Jean Van de Velde	73	74	70	75	292
Vijay Singh	72	72	67	70	281	José Rivero	76	80	70	66	292
Ian Woosnam	71	67	71	73	282	Frank Nobilo	72	75	74	72	293
Mark McNulty	73	73	67	71	284	Peter Fowler	73	74	77	69	293
Carl Mason	76	70	72	67	285	Paul Broadhurst	71	79	71	72	293
Jesper Parnevik	70	75	69	72	286	Per-Ulrik Johansson	77	71	72	74	294
Costantino Rocca	75	71	72	68	286	Joakim Haeggman	73	72	73	76	294
Retief Goosen	72	75	71	69	287	Peter Mitchell	76	77	70	71	294
Rodger Davis	74	74	70	69	287	Peter Baker	75	74	66	79	294
Miguel Angel Jiménez	73	70	75	69	287	Ian Palmer	76	74	75	70	295
Ernie Els	73	72	71	71	287	Andrew Oldcorn	72	75	75	73	295
José Coceres	74	73	70	70	287	Greg Turner	73	77	73	72	295
Paul Way	71	69	73	75	288	Roger Chapman	71	72	77	77	297
Anders Försbrand	72	75	72	69	288	Jim Payne	75	78	72	72	297
Barry Lane	73	74	73	68	288	Paul McGinley	76	73	77	71	297
Gordon Brand, Jr.	71	76	70	71	288	Ronan Rafferty	77	77	72	71	297
David Feherty	72	74	74	68	288	De Wet Basson	77	76	73	73	299
Howard Clark	72	74	75	68	289	Des Smyth	77	70	80	72	299
Sandy Lyle	78	70	70	71	289	Steven Richardson	77	77	74	71	299
Sam Torrance	74	70	71	74	289	Robert Karlsson	75	75	71	78	299
Bernhard Langer	72	71	74	73	290	Wayne Westner	77	73	75	74	299
José-Maria Olazabal	70	74	73	73	290	Jamie Spence	75	72	78	Withdrew	
Nick Faldo	74	70	75	72	291	Tony Johnstone	72	77	79	Withdrew	
Gary Orr	76	73	72	70	291	Stephen Ames	80	79	75	Withdrew	
Mark James	79	72	70	70	291	Brian Marchbank	82			Withdrew	

VALDERRAMA

27th-30th October 1994   Purse £750,000

	SCORES				TOTAL		SCORES				TOTAL
Bernhard Langer	71	62	73	70	276	Tony Johnstone	67	71	74	77	289
Vijay Singh	71	70	70	66	277	Peter Mitchell	65	74	74	76	289
Severiano Ballesteros	69	67	68	73	277	Peter Hedblom	71	70	75	74	290
Miguel Angel Jiménez	65	70	72	71	278	Anders Försbrand	73	66	75	77	291
Colin Montgomerie	69	65	72	72	278	Klas Eriksson	75	69	74	73	291
Mark McNulty	70	69	69	71	279	Mark Davis	74	68	73	76	291
Costantino Rocca	69	72	67	73	281	Pierre Fulke	68	71	79	74	292
Ian Woosnam	68	69	73	72	282	Phillip Price	71	76	72	73	292
José-Maria Olazabal	70	70	71	71	282	Greg Turner	75	70	69	79	293
Frank Nobilo	70	69	73	71	283	Gary Orr	75	69	75	74	293
Joakim Haeggman	71	71	69	73	284	Paul Way	70	73	77	73	293
David Gilford	70	74	69	71	284	Barry Lane	72	71	71	80	294
Sven Strüver	71	71	70	73	285	Rodger Davis	71	74	75	75	295
Mike Harwood	70	70	71	74	285	Jonathan Lomas	71	73	79	72	295
Howard Clark	71	71	70	73	285	Eduardo Romero	75	73	74	74	296
Nick Faldo	74	70	71	70	285	Paul McGinley	73	78	70	75	296
Per-Ulrik Johansson	72	75	64	74	285	Carl Mason	73	74	76	74	297
Robert Allenby	69	72	75	70	286	Andrew Coltart	71	76	74	76	297
Paul Curry	70	68	73	75	286	Russell Claydon	72	70	78	77	297
Darren Clarke	74	68	71	73	286	Gordon Brand Jnr.	74	69	79	76	298
Miguel Angel Martin	72	73	67	74	286	Philip Walton	75	71	77	76	299
Paul Eales	69	72	72	74	287	Ronan Rafferty	71	75	73	81	300
Sandy Lyle	71	72	69	75	287	José Rivero	79	75	78	69	301
Mark Roe	74	73	71	69	287	Gabriel Hjertstedt	77	75	76	74	302
Mark James	75	71	72	70	288	Retief Goosen	79	74	75	76	304
Sam Torrance	65	73	72	78	288	Lee Westwood	76	76	76	78	306
Jesper Parnevik	73	67	73	76	289	Wayne Westner	84	73	73	82	312

VALDERRAMA

CLUB COMPETITIONS AND MATCHES

(All monthly competitions are handicap.)

1986

January	Monthly Competition
Eduard Brandstrom	Stableford
March	**Monthly Competition**
John Fitzpatrick	Stableford
May	**Monthly Competition**
Jaime Ortiz-Patiño	Medal
Nancy Mohn	Stableford
July	**Monthly Competition**
Carla Maus	Stableford
August	**Monthly Competition**
Jaime Ortiz-Patiño	Medal
Luis Babiano	Stableford
September	**Monthly Competition**
Eduard Brandstrom	Medal
William Hoeveler	Stableford
October	**Monthly Competition**
Alexander Gut	Medal
Nancy Mohn	Stableford
November	**Monthly Competition**
Jaime Ortiz-Patiño	Medal
James Stewart	Stableford
December	**Monthly Competiton**
John Milln	Medal
David Naylor-Leyland	Stableford

1987

January	Monthly Competition
Umberto Neri	Medal
Jaime Ortiz-Patiño	Stableford
February	**Monthly Competition**
Antonio Fernandez del Villar	Medal
Wg Cdr. Patrick Stephenson	Stableford
March	**Monthly Competition**
Antonio Fernandez del Villar	Medal
Maxwell Neilson	Stableford
April	**Annual Championship**
Michael Gut	Scratch (men's)
Luis Babiano	Stableford (men's)
Nancy Mohn	Scratch (ladies')
Hildegard Steinbeck	Stableford (ladies')
November	**Monthly Competition**
Luis Babiano	Medal
Brian Lloyd	Stableford

VALDERRAMA

1988	
March	**Monthly Competition**
Garth S. Jones	Medal
James Stewart	Stableford
April	**Annual Championship**
Franz Türler	Scratch (men's)
Brian Lloyd	Stableford (men's)
Nancy Mohn	Scratch (ladies')
Monique Norton	Stableford (ladies')
May	**Monthly Competition**
Johanna Rosenthal	Medal
Paul Jeanty	Stableford
June	**Monthly Competition**
James Stewart	Medal
William Hoeveler	Stableford
July	**Monthly Competition**
Umberto Neri	Medal
Johanna Rosenthal	Stableford
August	**Monthly Competition**
Anthony Burridge	Medal
Barbara Rohleder	Stableford
September	**Monthly Competition**
Brian Lloyd	Medal
David Naylor-Leyland	Stableford

1989	
January	**Monthly Competition**
Luis Babiano	Medal
Johanna Rosenthal	Stableford
March	**Annual Championship**
Jeremy Caplan	Scratch (men's)
Anthony Hamilton	Stableford (men's)
Nancy Mohn	Scratch (ladies')
Franca Neri	Stableford (ladies')
June	**Monthly Competition**
Garry Cottam	Medal
Sir John Lawson	Stableford
July	**Monthly Competition**
Susanne Peyer	Medal
Susanne Stinnes	Stableford
August	**Monthly Competition**
Nancy Mohn	Medal
Paul Jeanty	Stableford
September	**Monthly Competition**
Dieter Bredemann-Lauff	Medal
Paul Jeanty	Stableford
December	**Monthly Competition**
Nancy Mohn	Medal
Ulf Skuncke	Stableford

VALDERRAMA

1990	
February	**Monthly Competition**
Peter MacEwen	Medal
Umberto Neri	Stableford
March	**Monthly Competition**
Nancy Mohn	Medal
James Stewart	Stableford
April	**Annual Championship**
Barry Stirling	Scratch (men's)
Edward Naylor-Leyland	Stableford (men's)
Nancy Mohn	Scratch (ladies')
Monique Norton	Stableford (ladies')
David Naylor-Leyland	Governor's Plate (seniors')
June	**Monthly Competition**
William Sykes	Medal
Axel Blikstad	Stableford
July	**Monthly Competition**
Axel Blikstad	Medal
William Sykes	Stableford
August	**Monthly Competition**
Anthony Burridge	Medal
Barry Stirling	Stableford
September	**Monthly Competition**
Barry Stirling	Medal
Dieter Bredemann-Lauff	Stableford
October	**Monthly Competition**
Brian Lloyd	Medal
Johanna Rosenthal	Stableford
December	**Monthly Competition**
Susanne Peyer	Medal
Siri MacEwen	Stableford

1991	
January	**Monthly Competition**
Axel Blikstad	Medal
Arthur Gilmour	Stableford
February	**Monthly Competition**
Brian Lloyd	Medal
Siri MacEwen	Stableford
March	**Annual Championship**
Jeremy Caplan	Scratch (men's)
Arthur Gilmour	Stableford (men's)
Johanna Rosenthal	Scratch (ladies')
Susanne Peyer	Stableford (ladies')
Ivor Binney	Governor's Plate (seniors')
May	**Monthly Competition**
Nancy Mohn	Medal
Axel Blikstad	Stableford
June	**Monthly Competition**
Axel Blikstad	Medal
Peter MacEwen	Stableford
July	**Monthly Competition**
Alf Blikstad	Medal
Paul Jeanty	Stableford
August	**Monthly Competition**
Edward Naylor-Leyland	Medal
Arthur Gilmour	Stableford
September	**Monthly Competition**
Arthur Gilmour	Medal
Paul Jeanty	Stableford
December	**Monthly Competition**
Nancy Mohn	Medal
Arthur Gilmour	Stableford

1992

January	**Monthly Competition**
Patricia Stirling	Medal
Barry Stirling	Stableford
February	**Monthly Competition**
Ivor Binney	Medal
Arthur Gilmour	Stableford
March	**Monthly Competition**
Arthur Gilmour	Medal
Peter MacEwen	Stableford
April	**Annual Championship**
Björn Ronning	Scratch (men's)
Anthony Hamilton	Stableford (men's)
Nancy Mohn	Scratch (ladies')
Susanne Peyer	Stableford (ladies')
Brian Lloyd	Governor's Plate (seniors')
June	**Monthly Competition**
Garry Cottam	Medal
Malcolm Morrison	Stableford
July	**Monthly Competition**
Joseph de Gruyter	Medal
Axel Blikstad	Stableford
August	**Monthly Competition**
Anthony Burridge	Medal
Barry Stirling	Stableford
October	**Monthly Competition**
Brian Lloyd	Medal
Barry Stirling	Stableford
December	**Monthly Competition**
Barry Stirling	Medal

1993

April	**Annual Championship**
Björn Ronning	Scratch (men's)
Hans Rosenthal	Stableford (men's)
Brenda McNeil	Scratch (ladies')
Waltraud Lloyd	Stableford (ladies')
Desmond Marriott	Governor's Plate (seniors')
Wg Cdr Patrick Stephenson	Senior Seniors'
September	**Monthly Competition**
James McNeil	Medal
Eduard Brandstrom	Stableford
November	**Monthly Competition**
María C. Stewart	Medal
Brian Lloyd	Stableford
December	**Monthly Competition**
Peter MacEwen	Medal
Siri MacEwen	Stableford

VALDERRAMA

1994	
January	**Monthly Competition**
Arthur Gilmour	Medal
Barry Stirling	Stableford
February	**Monthly Competition**
Nancy Mohn	Medal
Leslie Woodley	Stableford
March	**Monthly Competition**
James Stewart	Medal
María C. Stewart	Stableford
April	**Annual Championship**
Jeremy Caplan	Scratch (men's)
Leslie Woodley	Stableford (men's)
Siri MacEwen	Scratch (ladies')
Maria Concepción Stewart	Stableford (ladies')
Eduard Brandstrom Senior	Governor's Plate (seniors')
Lord Keith of Castleacre	Senior Seniors'
June	**Monthly Competition**
James McNeil	Medal
Brenda McNeil	Stableford
July	**Monthly Competition**
Barry Stirling	Medal
María C. Stewart	Stableford
August	**Monthly Competition**
Malcolm Morrison	Medal
Lincoln Bolsover	Stableford
September	**Monthly Competition**
Brenda McNeil	Medal
Siri MacEwen	Stableford

1995	
January	**Monthly Competition**
Bill White	Medal
Eduard Brandstrom	Stableford
February	**Monthly Competition**
Larry Cooper	Medal
Arthur Gilmour	Stableford
March	**Monthly Competition**
Ann Marie Zwanenburg	Medal
Larry Cooper	Stableford
April	**Annual Championship**
Jeremy Caplan	Scratch (men's)
Felipe Ortiz-Patiño	Stableford (men's)
Nancy Mohn	Scratch (ladies')
Johanna Rosenthal	Stableford (ladies')
Eduard Brandstrom	Governor's Plate (seniors')
Wg Cdr Patrick Stephenson	Senior Seniors'
May	**Monthly Competition**
Umberto Neri	Medal
Barry Stirling	Stableford

VALDERRAMA

VALDERRAMA

CHANGES TO THE COURSE

1st

New tees have been built and the green has been completely rebuilt to USGA specifications.

3rd

New tees have been built at the 3rd hole, lengthening this short Par-3.

4th

This hole has been completely rebuilt from tee to green. 70,000m³ of earth have been moved. New tees have been created. The hill in front at the first landing green has been lowered, and the ravine at the bottom of the tees filled in. The fairway which slanted from right to left has been raised. The lake that sat on the right of the green has been moved with the cascade coming down the hill into the lake, and a new green, further up the hill, has been built to USGA specifications, making this a challenging Par-5 which can be reached in two with a strong levante. The entrance is very narrow and a bunker has been created on the left of the green.

5th

New tees have been built, making this a challenging Par-4.

6th

New tees have been built and extra bunkers placed around the green which is now surrounded by six bunkers.

7th

This used to be a short Par-5 and has now been converted into a difficult Par-4. New tees have been built. Again, the fairway after the first landing area has been raised to avoid the balls rolling off into the ravine. A totally new green has been built to USGA specifications, and new bunkers have been placed around the green. Land behind the green has been acquired to increase the area for spectators.

8th

New tees have been built.

VALDERRAMA

9th

A mounding has been created behind the 9th green where the land used to fall off.

10th

The tees have been extended and rebuilt. A small lake has been built to the left of the fairway, which reserves the water from our wells as well as the water coming down from the 17th. This stream runs along the left side of the green. The water for the small lake goes into the big reservoir of 19,000m³ capacity. This reservoir used to be an unsightly ravine. We connected the big lake to the pump-house.

    We have done extensive planting of oleanders, bougainvillea and flowers around the reservoir to hide the service roads that go from Maintenance to the pump-house.

11th

We have brought in 50,000m³ of soil to raise the first landing area in order to stop the balls rolling off the fairway into a ravine. This hole used to be a very short Par-5 and has now been extended to a challenging Par-5 with a narrow entrance to the green and new bunkering. This extension was possible thanks to the extra land that had been acquired when we purchased the golf course from Sotogrande S.A. The land in question consisted of seven lots, four of which had been sold. The remaining three were still the property of Sotogrande S.A. and, luckily for us, none had been built on. The land and the access roads to service these plots were incorporated into the golf course, and the hill blocking the view of the sea from the Clubhouse and the 11th fairway was cut down. Earth was used to raise the first landing area of the 11th fairway.

12th

A new championship tee and the realignment of the other tees was carried out. The green was entirely rebuilt to USGA specifications.

13th

All the tees have been raised and reorientated for

better alignment with the fairway. By bringing the tees further back we have considerably lengthened the hole.

14th

New tees have been built. A new green has also been built to USGA specifications, and the bunkers around the green have all been redesigned.

15th

This hole has been extensively changed. New tees have been built thanks to the acquisition of the land referred to above. Also, a new green has been totally built to USGA specifications, and bunkers on the right have been extended.

16th

New tees have been built and the banks on the left of the green have been raised to accommodate spectators. We have also mounded the right of the green leading up to the 17th tees.

17th

This hole has been completely rebuilt from tee to green, and is now a challenging Par-5, slightly dog-legged to the right. New tees have been built. The fairway now rises to a plateau but then falls off to the lake in front of the green. Water from the lake runs down the left-hand side of the fairway before crossing over and ending up in the small lake to the left of the 10th. The water continues along the right-hand side of the green, which has been completely rebuilt to USGA specifications, with a large amphitheatre behind the green which can accommodate up to 7,000 spectators. The retaining wall on the right of the fairway is a gabion wall covered with bougainvillea, and also makes for a very good viewing area.

18th

The tees have been rebuilt and the hole has been lengthened. Substantial mounding has been created behind the green to accommodate a large number of spectators.

VALDERRAMA

PRACTICE FACILITIES

Two new practice putting greens have been built. We have also built a chipping green next to the driving range, with an apron and practice bunkers. The driving range itself has been raised with over 80,000m³ of earth, thus making it possible to see where your ball ends up. This earth movement has also made possible the rerouting of the service road under the driving range.

DRAINAGE

Proper drainage has been installed under all the tees that have been rebuilt, and an extensive amount of drainage has been installed in fairways throughout the course. All green side bunkers have been rebuilt with drainage.

AREAS AROUND GREENS

An area of between half an acre and one acre around each green has been seeded with creeping bentgrass or a mixture of creeping bentgrass and ryegrass. These areas have also been extensively drained.

CART PATHS

Cart paths have been built for golf carts along all Par-3s and also between the green and the tees of each hole.

SERVICE ROADS

An extensive network of service roads, including a tunnel under the driving range, has been constructed, leading from the pump house to the 12th and 13th greens. This same service road also runs under the 12th fairway. The old service roads that ran along the right of the 14th fairway and the right of the 16th fairway and behind the 15th green have now been eliminated to make room for the planting of trees.

PUMP HOUSE

An up-to-date pump house has been installed by the American firm, Carol Childers.

IRRIGATION

The new irrigation system was installed from wall to wall with over 5,000 sprinkler heads. Initially

VALDERRAMA

we installed a hydraulic system which has now been converted to a computerised Toro Network 8000. All the irrigation and all the machinery on the golf course is Toro, upgraded with their latest models.

PLANTING

Over 3,000 *Halipensis* pine trees have been planted around the property to shield the course and golfers from some villas which were built exceedingly close to the golf course. Over 500 olive trees, several hundred years old, have been transplanted to tie in with the native cork oak trees. Over 300 young (60 years old) cork oak trees have been planted between various fairways to continue a natural forest of cork oak trees.

SERVICE AREAS

A helipad has been built behind the practice chipping green. The area in the trees behind the pump house has been cleared to accommodate the medical centre. Three television platforms have been built: one in the ravine to the right of the driving range; a large one in the trees to the right of the 12th fairway, and the third has been dug out of the hill to the left of the 14th green. None of these three platforms is visible from the golf course. Six electric gates have been installed around the golf course to give access to the maintenance roads from the public road system.

MAINTENANCE AREAS

A completely new maintenance complex has been built between the 10th green and the 18th tees. A second maintenance area has been built in the woods to the right of the 6th fairway, where sand gravel and peat are stored as well as heavy equipment.

VALDERRAMA